# Scorekeeping

# Scorekeeping

## ESSAYS FROM HOME

### Bob Cowser, Jr.

The University of South Carolina Press

© 2006 Bob Cowser, Jr.

Published by the University of South Carolina Press
Columbia, South Carolina 29208

www.sc.edu/uscpress

Manufactured in the United States of America

15  14  13  12  11  10  09  08  07  06    10 9 8 7 6 5 4 3 2 1

**Library of Congress Cataloging-in-Publication Data**

Cowser, Bob.
  Scorekeeping : essays from home / Bob Cowser, Jr.
    p. cm.
  ISBN-13: 978-1-57003-652-1 (cloth : alk. paper)
  ISBN-10: 1-57003-652-7 (cloth : alk. paper)
  ISBN-13: 978-1-57003-653-8 (pbk : alk. paper)
  ISBN-10: 1-57003-653-5 (pbk : alk. paper)
    1. Cowser, Bob—Childhood and youth.  2. Tennessee—Biography.  I. Title.
  CT275.C8565A3 2006
  976.8'053092—dc22
  [B]                                                           2006016878

The epigraph for this book is from "Our Parents" from *Different Hours* by Stephen Dunn.
Copyright ©2000 by Stephen Dunn. Used by permission of W. W. Norton & Company,
Inc.

This book was printed on Glatfelter Natures Natural, a recycled paper with 50 percent
postconsumer waste content.

For My Parents

We try to say what happened in that first house
where we were, like most children, the only
needy people on earth. We remember
what we were forbidden, who got the biggest slice.
Our parents, meanwhile, must have wanted something
back from us. We know what it is, don't we?
We've been alive long enough.

Stephen Dunn, "Our Parents"

# Contents

# Acknowledgements

Many of these essays were written to stand alone, as it were, and appeared first in a variety of literary magazines. My thanks to *Creative Nonfiction,* the *Sycamore Review,* the *Sonora Review,* the *American Literary Review,* the *Palo Alto Review,* the *Distillery,* and *Brevity* for giving them a home in the first place and for permission to reprint them here.

I also want to thank people who supported the writing of these essays over the years (even when they didn't know it or mean to): Anne Giuntoli, Greg Kuzma, Gerry Shapiro, Grace Bauer, Robert Brooke, Bob King, Lee Martin, Paul Eggers, K. J. Peters, K. J. Weir, Sandy Yannone, Liz Ahl, Sherrie Flick, Chauna Craig, Joel Peckham, Jon Ritz and John McNally (Nebraskans), and Mary Hussmann, Natalia Singer, and Kerry Grant (Laurentians).

Of course the book would not exist without the sustained interest and support of Linda Haines Fogle of the University of South Carolina Press. Karen Elmore of the University of Tennessee–Martin Special Collections and Archives and Charlotte Ward of the St. Lawrence University English Department also provided vital assistance with the preparation of the manuscript. Many thanks, ladies.

I want to single out Laurentians Neal Burdick, Bill Bradley and Paul Graham for their generous reads of the final drafts of this manuscript. And my sister-in-law Jessie Scott, who took care of my children while I put the finishing touches on this manuscript and my wife did the same with townspeople's hair.

I certainly owe a debt of gratitude to my parents and siblings, so good-natured about becoming characters in this little book and in others. I hope they'll recognize this as our story.

And thanks finally to my wife, Candace, and our boys, Jackson and Mason, who put up with my many absences, physical and otherwise, during the completion of this project. Since we've settled in a northern New York village roughly the same size as that Tennessee town where I grew up, the questions I've raised here about smalltown boyhoods seem to have a renewed significance, so I had those three in mind while revising these. But then I always do.

# Scorekeeping

# Introduction

## *Answers May Vary*

The year I was to enter the third grade, my father moved us to East Haven, Connecticut, while he enjoyed a teaching exchange at Quinnipiac College for the academic year. A bit of an underachiever at my regular grade school in rural Tennessee, I placed a lot of pressure on myself to perform at the Momauguin Elementary that fall. I craved a fresh start. Yet I found myself consistently outdistanced by a scrawny, big-nosed girl named Rinell Bisi, a budding valedictorian type who had taken first place in the classroom spelling bee and in most of the other academic challenges our giant, bearded teacher, Mr. Wilcox, had placed before us.

By late spring, though, I *had* successfully completed one or two more SRA reading comprehension units than Rinell, judging from the chart on the wall above our lockers, and I was clinging to that. So the morning I found myself stumped, pardon the pun, by one of the questions in a forestry unit I'd just read ("What is your favorite tree?" I believe), I was desperate. I worried all morning, staring out the classroom window onto the new grass of the playing fields. As our class made its way back from lunch, while Mr. Wilcox was in the hallway talking to our red-faced principal, Mr. Fappiano ("Mr. Fat Piano," as he was known to the fifth-graders), I snuck ahead into the classroom and into Mr. Wilcox's desk to find the teacher's guide and copy the correct response. "Answers may vary," I read in the teacher's guide, and copied that phrase verbatim onto my answer sheet.

Mr. Wilcox invited my mother to school later that week to confront me about the issue, but neither adult could keep a straight face when they met me in the cafeteria. Cheating is bad and all, I know that, knew it then, but I've found myself falling back on that third-grade answer often as I composed the pieces in this book. Calling them essays (as opposed to stories, I guess) means that I consider them attempts, experiments in making meaning. It means that I raise big questions Bill Roorbach says I'm not obligated to answer with any real certainty (something I'm not sure I believe in very much anyway). Answers to these questions can only be provisional and may indeed vary.

Funny, my wife says, that what amounts to the story of my adolescence, a period she claims lasted well into my thirties, should make for such a short book, roughly the same length in words as the USA Patriot Act. But there you are. I began the first of these essays twelve years ago in a spartan studio apartment I was renting on West Wisconsin Avenue in Milwaukee while a graduate student at Marquette University. The apartment was near where Jeffrey Dahmer had devoured his victims shortly before I moved to the neighborhood. I printed the first drafts of what is now "The Heart Is a Dark Forest" on paper made from recycled topographical maps I'd bought at a stationery store in the Grand Avenue Mall. Maybe it was that paper, but I began this book with the misguided idea that it would be about place. Perhaps I thought it was my inheritance as a "Southern writer." Looking at these essays now, I see place gets but nominal attention, unless you consider "home" a place. And I'm afraid I can't rightly lay claim to a Southern inheritance, since I have not even retained the accent.

No, it's really a book about the nascent inner life I describe in this collection's title essay as that life we come to live beyond our bodies, perhaps inside our heads, as we come of age. And it's of course about people, curious survivals from my old life, Willa Cather would call them, some who've made the difficult passage through adolescence with me and some who survive only in memory. With the self at the book's center, the essays move out toward a galaxy of these "others"— parents, sisters, a younger brother, schoolmates, enemies, mentors. Often I work by comparison, laying my story alongside that of one of these other characters to reveal patterns and divergences or, by a kind of mirroring or reflection, looking deeply at the other in order to see the self more clearly. (William Kittredge says such stories are interesting only when in these reflections readers can also see themselves, and I hope that's the case here.)

The point is to trace constellations in this galaxy, to make order and meaning. Eudora Welty says that's the gift of the literary life, the sense of the continuities in our lives we gain from reading and writing stories, the knack we develop for finding in what she calls "the thick tangle" of our experience what thread or clear line persists—one explanation for why you'll find references to so many writers and stories in these pages.

How does that old Glen Campbell song go? "Country Boy, you got your feet in L.A. / But your mind's on Tennessee." I guess that's me, more or less. I'm learning to live with it.

CANTON, NEW YORK

OCTOBER 2005

# Scorekeeping

We live two lives: one restless in our bodies and one beyond that, which saves us. That's a fortune cookie platitude I came to all by myself the summer I finished eighth grade and turned fourteen, the summer my brother's grade-school friend took a revolver from his father's rifle cabinet and shot himself in the head. I knew it was a plain thought even as I composed it, lying on my back in my bed the nights after the kid killed himself. I had made it deliberately plain, piecing it together word by word. I did not want the echo of scripture to complicate what I thought was the barest truth of things.

This was 1984. My brother, Jimmy, and I lived with our family in the rural West Tennessee town of Martin, two hours up the Mississippi from Memphis, along the same stretch of the river Huckleberry Finn and another Jim are said to have traveled. Martin was a railroad town established in 1873 on land originally ceded from the Chickasaw and named for a William Martin, who donated considerable acreage in order that the Illinois Central tracks might be routed through the area's creek bottoms. A boy's life there was mostly slow but also oddly brutal, something our parents had not known to prepare my brother and me for, having transplanted themselves and their family to rural Tennessee from other places. But the hollow report of that revolver had jarred all of us into a new awareness. I struggled to get my mind around the notion of two lives at first, though it had been my own idea originally. I couldn't imagine in any detail a life beyond my bodily one, beyond the grief I found when I came to that body's limits. Maybe we don't find that place beyond our bodies until we are in dire need, which is the one time we can trust ourselves to learn anything, need being such a fine teacher.

Just what was going on in the larger world that summer I'm not sure. I always think how the sixties offers so many defining events—lunar landings, police actions, assassinations, and rock group breakups—that might serve as backdrop for the story of a life. The Chinese curse of interesting times. But this was the eighties, which most people I know can't yet think of as really being "the past," and history hasn't dignified us with any such curse. Even if I could put a finger on what the world was like when I turned fourteen, I know the people of Martin were not paying it any mind, were in fact resisting most of the larger world's conventions, time among them. To leave I-55 near Cairo, Illinois, and head east across the river into Tennessee on one of the ribbonlike two-lane country highways that intersects the interstate (which you have to do to find Martin) is at least to step out of time, if not to step back in it.

It is entirely possible that I never gave one thought to what was going on in the world beyond me that summer. I believed, right up to the time my brother's friend killed himself, that I had my own mess of a life to deal with. My seventh-grade history teacher had told me in front of our entire class that I was a "bad advertisement" for my parents, though I had tried, almost in spite of myself, to make myself presentable to the adults in my life. I was a compulsive talker, pudgy and flat-footed, who'd had braces cemented to my teeth the winter previous and who was quite bitter that at fourteen my body had begun, in so many ways, to betray me. When my eyesight started to go around that time, I took it for an omen, the last straw, salt in the wound.

My eyesight left me gradually at first. Earlier that spring, I had been unable to read the chalkboard from my desk in the last row of Mr. Cole's American history class. I did my best to explain that fact away and refused even to talk about the possibility of wearing glasses. "It's the glare,"

I told my parents. But I was also struggling that summer, as I always had, to play baseball, and Junior Babe Ruth ended the excuse-making abruptly. In my first seventeen at-bats that summer, I had either struck out or rolled weakly to the second baseman. I wasn't seeing the ball. It was like a cartoon aspirin whizzing toward me, and it was all I could do to chip it to the right side of the infield—the surest sign, my coach said, that a right-handed hitter is picking the ball up late.

"He's afraid of the ball," I heard Ronnie Powell tell the other grimy ballpark urchins between the pitches offered me. He stood behind the plate while I batted, his shirt open and his rakelike ribs pressing against the chain-link backstop. But he spoke the truth. I knew, standing in the soft clay of the batter's box, that the summer night loomed somewhere out past the infield, hung like a curtain, deep and velvet black and utterly beyond me. Base hits went out there, and I could hit nothing

*The ballpark at Rotary Field, corner of Christine and Clearwater Streets, Martin, Tenn., circa 1975, across the street from the author's home. Photograph courtesy of the Special Collections and Archives, University of Tennessee at Martin. Used by permission*

*Federal Land Bank T-Ball Team, Martin, Tenn., 1978. Author is kneeling in the lower right corner. Photograph courtesy of the Special Collections and Archives, University of Tennessee at Martin. Used by permission*

into that. I eventually broke down and made an appointment with my mother's optometrist, who told me that while I was not going blind, neither would my eyesight get any better—only gradually worse.

Rather than swing myself out of my slump, like the big-hearted boys in baseball novels I found in the juvenile section of the public library, I quit the team. The same week I quit, some of the older players on our team had held my friend Leland Bracknell down before practice and shoved a dead bird—a crow—in his mouth. This never happened in the baseball novels. The older boys had gone after Leland *particularly* be-cause he lost one or two fly balls in the ballpark lights the night before, but they went after him *in general* because he was from Chicago and was thus different, as in not like them. They chased him like rodeo handlers after a roping calf, around the bases and then in circles in the outfield. When they caught him behind one of the dugouts, Jeff Wright held his legs and Tom Jones his arms, while Rip Jones pried Leland's mouth open with one hand and stuffed the bird in it with the other. "Don't,"

Leland was saying. "Don't, Goddammit!" Leland's family had moved down from Chicago when he was four or five, and Leland brought quite a mouth with him. He shouted curses that day that I had never heard before. Chicago curses, I was sure.

It was hard to watch Leland writhe there in the red dirt of the bullpen pitcher's mound, the bird's beak disappearing into the dark of his throat. I walked into one of the dugouts. The Bracknells lived in a brown mobile home just below our backyard, and Leland visited our house every day, so that he became like family. He would have come over more often, my mother used to joke, but for another neighbor's wire pen full of yelping Dobermans that stood between Leland's yard and ours. My parents drove him to every baseball practice and to all the games, and though they would never say so, I think they grew to love him. I didn't particularly like Leland. In many ways he frightened me. But he fascinated me too. Chicago seemed terribly exotic to me then, and Leland loved to regale me with stories about it, particularly about the food you could get there and the greasy delicatessens where you bought the food—Reuben sandwiches and meatball subs, dripping with sauce. Martin had no delicatessens. "Someday, we'll take the train up there," Leland would tell me. I suppose he was (aside from my brother) the closest thing I had to a real friend when I was fourteen, and as I get older I am beginning to realize that actually liking our friends is a luxury not all of us can afford.

Leland did not wait for a ride home that last day but walked alone before practice ever began. I stayed for practice that afternoon, but I was so sick to my stomach I could hardly hold a bat.

I returned to Harmon Field only once more, several days later. As a means of making my quitting official, I had my mother drive me to the field an hour or so before one of our games so I could surrender my uniform. It was early evening, the players' shadows still long on the infield as they warmed up. I dragged myself toward my coach, who stood in the gravel on-deck circle near the visitors' dugout, about a hundred yards from where my mother parked. He was a tire builder out at the Goodyear plant, a strong man but quite short. Over my shoulder I slung the green uniform my mother had cleaned and pressed and placed on a clothes hanger.

On the drive from our house to the field, Mom and I had rehearsed an honorable bit, about quitting and being sorry for leaving the coach shorthanded, and upon reaching him, I delivered it by rote. "Be respectful," my mother had said to me as I climbed out of our Gran Torino wagon, "even if you have to fake it." I heard her even as I talked. It went rather well, all in all, though I don't remember a word of what I said. It probably lasted all of forty-five seconds.

The coach's rhetoric came next. "If I had a body like you, hell, son," he said, exasperated, "I could push houses over." He didn't say anything else, his eyes fixed on some distant point beyond outfield fence. I wasn't listening anyway. That kind of talk had always seemed full of riddles to me. I hung the curved neck of the clothes hanger carefully in the chain link of the high dugout fence, so that the breezes blowing around the ballpark caught the uniform from time to time, holding the pants aloft like a long, green flag. Then I turned from him and walked toward my mother's car, thinking only of the maggoty crow in Leland's mouth.

"Do you think I'm a wimp, Mom?" I asked matter-of-factly as I got back in the car.

"No," she said, turning the Torino on and beginning to drive away. "Leland will always remember that you were loyal."

It made me uneasy, the way my mother treated my quitting like a principled *non servium*. I hadn't quit as much out of loyalty to Leland as I had out of a well-founded fear that the fate that befell him would befall me if I continued to play, and I guess my mother knew it. But it was her way to offer her children alternative perspectives to the choices they made, "enlightened" perspectives, she called them. She told me that she understood my decision to give the game up, that in an odd way she was proud of me for quitting, and she took the opportunity presented by my predicament to tell me once again what a literally god-forsaken place she thought Martin was. Life there was so unlike her upbringing in suburban Cleveland, an upbringing that she could represent as humble (they were poor) or remarkably dignified, depending on her rhetorical needs at the time. "I'll lay a bet they never fed crows to the students at the St. Augustine Academy for girls," my dad might say to her, quite sincerely. "No, Bob, they didn't," she would tell him, leaving the room or closing a door or lighting a cigarette for emphasis. My dad had grown up in rural Hopkins County, Texas, where people did things like stuff crows in boys' mouths and feed meat mined with shards of glass to family dogs, so he deferred to Mom on matters of civility.

I was more or less resigned to the quitting. I never bought, and still don't buy, any of that crap about quitters never winning, though I think I hear it about once a day. I searched earnestly in those years for words that I might live by, accepting no proverb without testing it against others I put my faith in. The line of bullshit about quitting directly contradicts a pair of aphorisms I clung to tightly, out of necessity more than anything: that I couldn't "win them all," and consequently that, as my mother had always said and said again that day, I had to "pick my battles."

Still, a part of me hated to quit baseball, growing up as I had in a house immediately next to Martin's little league park on Christine Street. I knew I stunk at baseball, but I hadn't always. Baseball was one thing I had grown up expecting to do. My family had always supped in summer over the din of infield chatter across the street. "Batter, batter, batter," the boys sang—then "SWING," and then we heard the crack of the bat or the percussion of the catcher's mitt. The sound of that chatter was maddening sometimes—it was supposed to be, like a plague of singing locusts. Yet on quiet Wednesday nights, when all of Protestant Martin was at church (we Cowsers were one of the few Catholic families in town) and no games were played, especially toward the end of the summer and the little league season and the beginning of school, my brother and I stood in the front yard and guessed the silence of the empty park was the loneliest sound we had ever heard, and wished for the chatter to come back.

I was in free fall after that. There was no life for a boy in Martin who wasn't playing baseball. The game brings a young life order, not just the scheduled games and practices but the game itself. There is an order in it, an order transcending clocks and time. Even the act of pitch and catch connected me to something, to someone beyond myself. But I had turned my back on that. Instead, I woke late in the day, after my parents had gone to teach summer school and my sister Mary had taken off for band practice and my sister Ruth for babysitting, after my brother left on his bike to do whatever it was that cool boys did in summer (I, of course, had no idea). The house was dark when I crawled from bed—my parents kept lights off in the summer to keep the house cool—and I would haunt the place until the family returned, sneaking frozen mini-donuts and half-frozen Girl Scout cookies from the deep freeze and watching baseball and reruns and soap operas on television. We got Cubs and Braves games on cable. I think my dad was very worried about me, because he followed me around with suggestions about what I might do with myself. He'd not done that before. "Go to the library" was one suggestion he made over and over, just to give you an idea.

Some evenings, Leland and his "chain-ganger friends," as my prim sister Ruth liked to call them, showed up at our back door to urge me outside into the streets with them. And some nights I went, up Clearwater to McGill Street then up Summer Street, where the nice girls lived in the old homes. Leland played Quiet Riot on his boom box while we walked down the middle of those quiet streets with a generic but very real sort of defiance. Now that all that's passed and I've pretty much abandoned Leland, my sister laughs and asks me if I can believe I was a chain-ganger. I don't know, but I guess I can believe it.

I had the vaguest sense of dread about my life then. High school waited for me at the end of the summer like something big and messy and difficult, something that counted and would matter later in my life. I was not ready for things that mattered. That sense creeps back into my life from time to time even today, with particular frequency since I got married and took a full-time teaching job: the sense that though I appear thirty-five, I am in fact still only fourteen on the inside and am biding my time until someone in a position of authority figures me out. Now I have some perspective and can see life beyond my "permanent

*The author's brother, Jimmy, in his Little League (Martin Bank Astros) uniform, 1984. From the author's family collection*

record," but in those awkward years I could not see beyond my school days to a better time, and had only my parents' word that such a time would ever come.

I did quit baseball in enough time to reclaim my position as score-keeper and announcer for the little league next door. The summer before, for seven dollars a game, I'd sat in a makeshift press box keeping official score and announcing the batters for the pee-wee league games. "Now batting so-and-so," I would say. "So-and-so on deck." Occasionally I'd vary things a little, add something I picked up from all the baseball I watched on television. But the parents and coaches grumbled when I did that.

The job seemed to fit me, like nothing else in my life. The money was fine for a boy my age, "walking around money," Mom called it, and I could work alone, which seemed important at the time. The job also involved pretty much constant talking. And the fact that my little brother, Jim, played baseball so well made the job rewarding in other ways. Jimmy had moved up to little league that summer, to the Argo Collier Astros, and he had taken up pitching. It seemed no one could hit him. Pee-wee players batted against a pitching machine, but little leaguers faced a live arm, and Jim had discovered since moving up that his arm was very live.

While most of the other boys threw overhand, Jimmy brought side-arm pitching back to the Martin Little League, and all the little league fathers agreed he was something to watch. He would bring his arms and striding leg very close to his body as he began his windup, then dip his shoulder deeply so that he held the ball just above the ground. He released the ball from that point—about seven o'clock—as he brought his arm whiplike across his body and stepped toward the plate, often with such force that the cap popped off his head. The sun setting orange behind him (as it often did on those evenings), Jim must have appeared to the young hitters an illusionist. There was sleight of hand to what he did. I loved to watch the strikeouts line up as I recorded them on the

*The author under the kitchen window of the family home, at 120 Virginia Street, Martin, Tenn., among his mother's tulips, probably Easter Sunday circa 1980. From the author's family collection*

score book's tiny baseball diamonds, K after K. I wrote them carefully, deliberately.

In a real way, Jim's pitching made my summer, the simple beauty of it, and I know it pleased my parents too. They no longer walked across Virginia Street to the ballpark as they had done faithfully the years I struggled through little league; Jim had become too superstitious and forbade them to come. But on the nights he was slated to pitch, Mom and Dad would pull lawn chairs out under the giant magnolia in our side yard to sit amid the fireflies and watch their boy throw. He was too dazzling to miss. It is ennobling to do even the smallest thing well and gracefully, and Jim's dedication to pitching and sheer skill at doing it taught me that, though I don't think I quite understood it that summer. And I found real satisfaction in witnessing and recording my brother's grace. It connected me to the game and its order, though, again, it has taken me some years to figure that out.

The night we found out about the suicide, I was across the street working a ball game. My mother and father were both waiting for me to return from the ballpark. It was odd for my father to be up that late—eleven or so. I found both my parents' faces in the porch's lamplight. Hearing it open, they had both started for the door.

"Alex Lee has killed himself," my dad said coolly as I walked past him. "Shot himself." I stopped dead. Dad took it upon himself to be the head of the house in times like that—not in a loud way, but diplomatically, almost reluctantly. I always heard more duty in his voice than anything.

Mom explained that Jimmy had been told. "Take it easy with him," she said. Mom and Dad were going to do that. They did not know how he would take it. I suppose it is a story how he *did* take it.

Jimmy and this kid were fourth-grade classmates. I had only met my brother's friend a few times. He was blond and blue-eyed, smallish and still cherubic, a compulsive talker like myself, and beautiful, like my brother. Jimmy thought he was terribly funny, which threatened me somehow. His father was a successful auctioneer, one of the most prominent men in our county. As the son of schoolteachers, my brother had nothing in common with the dead boy. But both boys were bright and clever and, most of all, convinced of their toughness. That made them friends. Many days after school, the two boys had gone to his father's realty office on one of Martin's main drags, where they had gotten into liquor cabinets and all other sorts of mischief. Jim had never gotten in much trouble at home for any of that, and my brother pretty much gave up drinking altogether by the time he was thirteen, jaded as he was. But we learned later that his friend had paid dearly.

The day he shot himself, Alex had received his final fourth-grade report card. I never heard what the grades were, but at eleven, this child was convinced that he would rather be dead than wait for the rope-whipping he was sure he had earned at his father's hand. Before his father returned from work, he took one of his father's many revolvers, closed his mouth around it, and delivered himself from his body. My mother's friends say it was the father who found his body a few hours later and who, of those who survived the boy, was most wounded by that shot, most confused. The words "Mouth of the South" were chiseled into the back of his gravestone. His father insisted on that.

I do not recall If I slept at all the night I found out. I met my brother in the kitchen the next morning. He was slopping through a bowl of Corn Pops at the kitchen table.

"Dad bought the wrong goddamned cereal," he said to me vacantly. He had a mouth like Leland's, even then. I went for a bowl in a cupboard behind Jim. He became gravely serious then.

"I can't pitch, Bobby," he said to me, in a sadder voice than I ever heard from him. "I can't pitch, man."

And indeed he could not. A photographer from the *Weakley County Press* snapped him on the mound later that night, and the *Press* ran the photo in the lower right corner of the front page a week later. Jim is striding toward the plate in the picture, his red stirrup socks out of his shoes and flying and his cap about to pop from his head. He is a beautiful boy, but he is tired and grieved, with a man's grief. You can see that.

It would be poetic for me to tell you here that it was his friend's death that ruined Jim as a pitcher. It may be so. I only know Jim was not the same pitcher after that night. What had made him a good pitcher remained. But what had made him beautiful, an illusionist, was gone.

In fact, he was an altogether different boy after that gunshot. A few nights after Alex died, the police woke my parents very late to say they had my brother in a squad car, that he looked very bad, like he hadn't slept, and that they'd found him pacing one of the ballpark's dugouts across the street an hour or so before. The police thought he was much too young to be out at that hour. Jimmy told my parents the dead boy had come and "talked to him" that night, and that he'd snuck out the window and gone to the dugouts to think a while. I still don't know if he believed his friend, dead four days by then, had appeared to him, or if he'd made it up to save his skin. I would put almost nothing past my brother. I do know he hadn't slept in four days because I had been awake myself at all hours of the night, lying face up in my bed, and I had heard my brother banging around the house.

Jimmy never played baseball another summer but began to take odd jobs during the summer months instead—scrubbing 18–wheelers, bailing and hauling hay, painting houses. He became more like a boarder in my mother's home than a brother or a son. Jimmy still ate with us and allowed my mother to make his bed and wash his clothes. He bore us no ill will. Jim was still preternaturally cool. But some part of my brother became solemn. Not gloomy, simply solemn and reverent in the most natural way. The experience of his friend's death set Jim apart, and he could no longer consider himself a part of our family, and sometimes he said as much. There was a span of years around that time, in fact, during which my brother appeared in no family pictures. He had carved out a space next to himself, so that for a time there was no room for us. I think now that space was Alex's place, where my brother kept him. I cannot begrudge him that space, all things considered. He was looking for that place beyond his body. We were all doing that.

Certainly my brother had learned to do so from our father, who always allowed life to happen at one or two removes from himself. I lived my whole life with the sensation that my father was one room away, behind a half-closed door in a farther room, enjoying a silence and stillness I could never approximate. He walked every night up and down the wide streets around our house for the hour or so before my mother served dinner, and as I grew up I had always guessed he was visiting on those walks the people he kept closest to himself, the colorful characters from his Texas hometown that he told us about: his parents and dead siblings. For many years I misunderstood this. I sometimes thought he hadn't gotten the family he had bargained for, that he would have enjoyed having one of the quieter, more studious boys in my class for a son. But he'd lived a whole life, more than thirty-five years, before we came along, and he knew grief before he knew us. I know now it tempered him. My brother had joined my father in that farther space, for a while at least, and, ironically, I began to understand them both a little better.

I spent a lot of the time I was alone in our house the rest of that summer with my hands in my father's top drawer. He kept a roll of quarters there among his undershirts. I often stole two and rode Jim's bike or my sister Mary's down the hill and through the yards behind our house—not pedaling, just coasting—past the frothing Dobermans and Leland Bracknell's trailer to the Akin-Jackson Motor Company on the Dresden Highway, where I would buy a Pepsi. My father must have known I was taking the quarters, almost two a day, but he never said a word. One afternoon about two months after my brother's friend died, I found in that drawer a poem my father had written and titled "On the Suicide of an Eleven Year Old." Dad had just begun to publish poems then. I think he was fifty-one. Journals that included his work began to appear unannounced around the house, but I had never thought to read them. This poem I read, because I felt a part of it.

> Though we were told he was a hunter,
> Skilled already in the use of firearms
> (We know he held the pistol true),

Much game survived the boy's brief career.
The squirrels and the grey dove
Continued their feeding
Hours after the sudden shot,
And the doe is grazing now
Near the cedar brakes.
On that night the Earth
Did not waver from its course
Nor was the moon's ring related
To the grief we endured.

How still and perfectly the words lay there. I wanted to follow my father around the house and quote him to himself. "'The grief we endured': yes, Dad, yes! Perfect." Here was my dad scorekeeping, after all, ordering his grief. This—writing—was the small, ennobling thing he did, alone and quietly. I was on fire to talk to him about it but thought better of doing so.

Months later, that poem appeared in the *Sulphur River Review,* and though it has been years since he wrote it and though he has written much more in the meantime, I remain convinced it is the best thing my father ever wrote. I realize it is odd for a boy to say he was raised by a poem, even a hundred poems, but the fact that my own place in the world was made clearer to me precisely as I discovered that poem is, I insist, no coincidence. Readers can understand what I mean: what writers you love have said of the world must frame experience for you in some small sense, must have become a part of what life is. So it was for me.

My dad's poems taught me to honor—if not wholly love—space and distance. Their words are so still, so precise, move so close to what we all feel that I despair of them coming closer. Then the words ebb away, as if they respect the distance between themselves and what Dad means, and wants them to mean. It seems the poem pulled me out of that awful year, allowed me to compose myself. I found, or made, a life beyond my body. After that summer, I thought it no longer necessary that my father fill the spaces we sometimes found between us with talk, talk that must have seemed to him so idle. He loves and grieves in measured tones.

My brother has not written about the suicide yet, and he may never do it. For Jim life is its own calling. Jim had more of the boy than Dad or I did and so has kept that solemn place next to himself empty for his friend, as it should be. It is a division of labor: life happens to Jim; I do the scorekeeping.

# Hiatus

*How did things go wrong? Which is of course the oldest story....*

William Kittredge, "Taking Care"

I turned three years old right around the time my hometown of Martin, Tennessee, turned one hundred, in July 1973. This coincidence is remarkable chiefly because I was awarded the prize for best costume in the centennial parade staged that Fourth of July. Of course I don't remember winning the ribbon, but my mother has marked it as a sort of family milestone.

Several years ago now, I swiped my mother's reel-to-reel home movies from a shelf in our den where they'd sat fifteen years—we owned a camera but not a projector—and had them transferred to video. She had forgotten altogether what was on them, and I had teased myself for a long time with thoughts of the images those reels held. As the family screened the tape over the holidays, we were delighted, my mother particularly, to find from one of the original reels flickering footage of the centennial parade, including a few brief shots of my blue-ribbon costume. I am wearing a blue construction-paper hat and a nondescript

*View of Lindell Street, Martin, Tenn., circa 1985. Photograph courtesy of the Special Collections and Archives, University of Tennessee at Martin. Used by permission*

white shirt, carrying a construction-paper flag in one hand and holding my blue knickers up with the other, tripping over my sandaled feet as the parade moves along Lindell Street. My mother has always insisted that I won the prize that hot afternoon not for my costume but because I couldn't keep my pants pulled up over my abnormally small behind and had to stop all along the parade route to adjust myself, to the delight of the judges.

Sadly, that July afternoon was the high watermark of my relationship with my hometown. It seemed to sour year by year, so that by the time I left Martin to go to college in 1988 I was convinced the people there were hinting it was time I leave. In a dark moment recently, I read some of the inscriptions in my high school yearbooks. There is the stuff you'd expect: "To a wild and crazy guy," say, or "To a great friend." And that odd language you find nowhere else except in yearbooks, constructions like "LYLAB" (Love you like a brother), and "U R 2 cool 2 B 4—Gotten" (never forgetting people and things from high school is a note that's hit hard here, a kind of premature nostalgia). But I noted something else lurking in the notes my classmates wrote in my yearbook as well. Penne Pate wrote, "To a nice guy who is always pestering me." "To a sweet guy who gets a little pesty sometimes," wrote Penne's best friend, Tina Pinkleton, having perhaps read Penne's inscription. Christy Shore signed "to an intelligent pest in my homeroom." DoRann Killebrew sugarcoated the same message: "you make this school go crazy," she wrote, adding enthusiastically, "but that's good!" DoRann's reassuring afterthought was lost on me at the time. As far as I was concerned, the girls who signed my yearbook may as well have written, "you're from a different planet."

I was, after all. The planet Connecticut. My family and I were transplants to rural Tennessee from north of the Mason-Dixon, and like any transplants we had our struggles with rejection. Which isn't to deny or

*The author outside the family home at 176R Cosey Beach Avenue, East Haven, Conn., autumn 1978. From the author's family collection*

excuse the fact that, at bottom, I was a pest. I was excitable and talked constantly, to other people and to myself. My teachers marked the "talks too much" column on my report card every grading period, called my parents in more than once for parent-teacher conferences to talk about the talking problem. So I was a pest by nature. But I know my extra-terrestrial-ness made my personality all the more unappealing.

Competing theories exist about how my family ended up in Martin. There was the strictly economic imperative, the explanation I imagine my father would offer if you pressed him: he simply needed a better job. My parents met while teaching English together at Quinnipiac College in Hamden, Connecticut. She was thirty, he thirty-five. My mother told me once that by the time they met, she had thought to herself that she'd probably never marry. Dad must have thought that way too. They were engaged a few weeks after their first date, married only a few months after that, then bought a lovely little two-story white Cape Cod in North Haven. My older sister was born the next year. A storybook, really.

But after I arrived in the summer of 1970, things began to get tight financially. A small branch of the University of Tennessee, located in Martin, happened to be hiring English professors for that fall term. The salary was a huge chunk more than Dad had made in Connecticut, even more than that when you factored in the difference in cost of living. Martin offered my father the job he was looking for.

Then there's the more romantic explanation, one my mother (embittered and cynical, mind you, about the whole move) has suggested to me but one I have never heard my dad own up to: that my father moved us to Martin with hopes that he might buy a small farm outside of town and grow a few things, tend some cows and chickens. Dad wanted to rusticate, Mom says, play the poet-farmer—like Robert Frost in New Hampshire. My dad grew up on a small farm in rural East Texas and may have thought he wanted to go back to that life in some token manner.

None of that worked out once we got to Martin, though. In the interest of the children, my parents bought a large one-story house in town, near the elementary school and the city pool and the ball fields. It's just as well. I can't picture my dad farming any more than I can picture myself doing it, or helping him. My dad is smallish, bookish, not in the least handy. He once left a lawn mower running in the yard because he couldn't manage to turn it off, walking into the house instead to wait for the mower to run out of gas. When the same small push mower caught fire later that summer, he called the fire department, which sent a huge engine over to put it out. It seems the traits that made my father's father such an able farmer and businessman skipped at least a generation.

Still, Martin should have made us happy. In December 1970, four months after my parents moved there, *Esquire* magazine named Martin one of nine happy towns left in America. "There remain to this day communities in America where the kids look like the ones Norman Rockwell used to paint," the *Esquire* article begins, "pockets of small-town tranquility where the stomach of a cultivated man can recover from the lifelong ingestion of raw gobbets of modern civilization." No modern civilization to be found in Martin, that's for sure. In towns like Martin, the magazine rhapsodized, said civilized man could escape "noise, bus exhausts, dirt, rudeness, $400 apartments, $4 plastic business lunches, insolent taxi drivers, blackouts, riots, crime waves, people jams, and other incontrovertible evidence of the end of the world." Martin still boasts of its happy place status in its chamber of commerce literature now, some thirty-five years later.

Of course, the article cautions that "one may have to suppress liberal politics among deeply conservative neighbors, or overlook the Waspish self-regard of a town pleased to have no minorities," but asks if this is really "too high a price to pay?" I marvel at the way this last question is tossed off, like any such rhetorical question—"is it too much to ask?" Small-town, Waspish self-regard is easily overlooked from high-rises in New York, less easily so from houses next door. I get the impression that the writer of the *Esquire* piece never had to ask that question in a situation in which it wasn't strictly rhetorical, a situation where his immediate future and the futures of his children hung in the balance. The fates placed my parents in that very position, and they went for the Rockwell.

I sometimes think my dad, as a practically lifelong Texan, might have known better. And he may have felt right at home in a town like Martin, enjoyed it there. I tried to draw him out recently during a phone conversation about why we stayed in Martin as long as we did when it seemed everyone was so unhappy there, and why he never complained about Martin the way my mother did. "You need to remember I had a job there in Martin which I loved," he told me. It was all he would say on the matter.

That fact being established, I suppose my dad could deal with the rest. Repressing liberal politics, for instance, isn't a problem for my dad, who seems to practice repression and avoid confrontation by his very nature. But my mother has been nothing if not vocal on the subject of Martin. She loathes it. A native of Cleveland, my mother, in her Irish stubbornness, never made the adjustment to rural Southern life, even attempted it. She left everything she knew behind to make the move, including a tenured position at Quinnipiac and an unfinished Ph.D. at the University of Connecticut.

She says our initial years in Martin weren't so awful, that in fact the first ten years of her marriage were the happiest of her life. We children were toddlers in those years, darling and precocious, winning costume contests and performing in ballet recitals, saying interesting and clever things in the checkout line at Big Star. She glowed with love and simple pride. It wasn't until we started school that things went wrong.

I mostly just wanted to please my teachers at Martin Elementary, to fascinate and impress them. But I couldn't help myself from talking, to both teachers and students, and spent a lot of time in the hall or in the corner or at the chalkboard with my nose in a small circle. For all the class time I missed, I felt fortunate to receive my high school diploma at the end of things. It wasn't as though I was fearless as to the consequences of my misbehavior. Corporal punishment was held over the heads of the children at Martin Elementary, boys and girls alike, as the nasty fate that would befall all behavior problems: smart alecks, roughhousers,

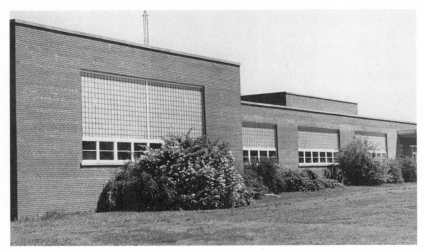

*The old Martin Elementary School Building, 1973 (since demolished). Photograph courtesy of the Special Collections and Archives, University of Tennessee at Martin. Used by permission*

*The Big Star Supermarket, University Street, Martin, Tenn., circa 1965. Photograph courtesy of the Special Collections and Archives, University of Tennessee at Martin. Used by permission*

playground pugilists, nap-time bed wetters, talkers, and gum chewers. It was supposedly available as a last resort, but it was practiced by teachers more as the rule than the exception. By and large the community supported the practice. Even now, when a worried parent voices an objection in a letter to the local paper's editor, a farmer will write in righteously the following week to declare, in effect, that his teachers beat the holy hell out of him and that he turned out just fine. In fact, he remembers that he rather liked it.

That paddling was swift and efficient explains some of its popularity, but I think it was the favorite mode of discipline mostly because it offered frustrated teachers a rush of physical satisfaction, a way of getting their hands on us. My teachers modified the paddles they hit us with —boards an inch thick and more than a foot long—as though they were pinewood derby cars. One teacher drilled holes through his paddle for improved aerodynamics, another wrapped silver duct tape around his to increase the concussion on our behinds, and still another had his unruly charges sign the paddle once he'd made them its victims. Even our otherwise demure female teachers had paddles, usually gifts from an education sorority they'd joined as coeds. All these paddles had names— names like "The Widow-maker," "The Reckoning," and "Peacekeeper" —and left distinct impressions on our bottoms and our young characters.

I remember a rumor that the principal of our school, Mr. Dunn, kept an electric paddle in his office that he reserved for real hard cases, reform-school types. One of the standing rules in our school was that any student sent to the hall and then found there by Mr. Dunn while he made his daily rounds received five licks, no questions asked. I spent a great deal of time waiting in those dank corridors, whimpering and mumbling, trying to somehow dissolve into the painted cinder blocks at the sound of approaching footsteps. This electric paddle even made its way into our schoolboy games: my sadistic friend Dwightie Wikstrom (another transplant whose family had moved to Martin from Minnesota) convinced me to play "electric paddle" with him and his older brother Lorne, a game that involved Lorne beating me about the buttocks and legs with a Wiffle ball bat while Dwight made a faint whirring sound through his nose. "I hope you've learned your lesson," Lorne would say intermittently in his principal voice. Lorne didn't hit hard; the point of the game was the absolute terror we felt even in invoking the name of that mythic paddle. "It doesn't hurt on the outside," my little brother had said at home on the occasion of his first real paddling, "it hurts on the inside."

When Jim had started school a few years after me, teachers regularly asked him if he was my brother, a question to which he replied proudly in the affirmative. "Nothing to be proud of," the teachers would reply curtly. Though these remarks were intended to put him in his place, on his guard, my brother seemed to take them as direct challenges to his boyhood and slights on the family honor, of which he had appointed himself defender from a very early age. He answered these challenges with a mischief that took on a whole other dimension from mine, one of defiance. He considered his childhood occupied territory and became a kind of a grade-school commando.

When he was five, a county constable carried Jimmy to our front door by his ear and told my parents he'd caught the boy throwing cucumbers at the county cruiser as it passed our yard on Virginia Street. The Halloween he was six, while my parents had our family trick-or-treating at one of the local college's dorms, my brother reported that he'd found a straight pin in a piece of caramel. The campus police had called the Hershey Company in Pennsylvania and shipped the caramel off to a lab in Memphis before Jimmy, sickened by conscience, confessed it was a ruse. Having so little success with the frontal cucumber attack, I guess, my brother had turned to more-covert, guerrilla operations. Our teachers thought he was a monster. I knew he simply had a highly developed sense of the injustice of childhood and felt compelled to defy openly teachers and other adults whom he found wanting. My mother, sympathetic as she was to his position, had a hard time reigning him in.

In fact, my mother never left either of our sides for a moment during our troubled childhoods, never doubted us when the matter was trouble at school, even when she should have. I was only paddled a few times, but a paddling was a weekly occurrence for my brother—he once got three paddlings in one day—and my mother wrote letters of outrage to the school board each time one of us was touched, letters that scared the board to death and earned her audience after audience with the superintendent and county attorney, who feared she'd sue. After such an audience, our teachers often mocked us as we walked down the dark halls of the school. "Better not paddle him," one might say to another, "his mommy will get us." She would have gotten them one way or another, though. They knew it, and so did we. I would have loved to attend just one of those audiences, watch my mother inhale deeply on one of the Marlboros she smoked, exhale hard, then let the school board have it. She was convinced that it wasn't her children that were the problem but the place itself, which she said made small, hardened things out of little boys.

Once a month my mother drove Jimmy and me to a renowned allergist in Jackson, Tennessee, fifty miles away, who told her my irritability and excitability in school were easily explained by my profound allergies to dust and mold, both of which were everywhere in the ancient Martin Elementary building. I think my mother clung mightily to that, to the idea that my problems had some external cause. My psychologist sister, Ruth, has since called us "permissively reared children" from a "child-centered home," but I don't know about any of that.

Recently, I brought back from a trip to my parents' home a letter my father's father, Grandad, wrote me just as I was learning to write myself, which my parents had retrieved from his things after he died and which I had wanted as a keepsake. My grandfather wrote in response to a letter I had written him the year I turned six and learned to spell. But I also found tucked in the envelope a note my mother wrote my grandfather to thank him for answering my letter. I had just loved getting it, she tells him in her letter, and she writes about the other babies, how smart they were and how big they were growing.

Then, oddly, she moves on to write about news my parents were awaiting from the NEH. My dad had applied for a grant that would have afforded the family eight weeks in Gainesville, Florida, that summer while my dad studied, and Mother wrote that my parents expected to hear any day. I knew how little she talked to my grandfather, and it struck me as odd that she would be so candid. My dad didn't get the grant, of course, and the lost note was the first I'd ever heard of a summer in Florida, but it broke my heart to see my mom's desperate wish to leave Martin laid so bare on that page, and to know as well that it didn't come true.

The note makes me wonder if my dad wasn't querying schools and grant foundations furiously during those years for even a temporary way out of town. After about ten years in Martin, my mother was finally delivered, at least for a while: one of my parents' former colleagues from Quinnipiac College had agreed, God knows why, to a teaching

*View of Long Island Sound from the second floor porch at 176R Cosey Beach Avenue, winter 1978. The author's brother, Jimmy, appears in the lower left corner. From the author's family collection*

exchange that would send him to UT Martin for nine months and send us packing back to Connecticut. Mom insisted that we spend our time in Connecticut on the beach, so family friends scouted houses right on Long Island Sound. My parents ultimately decided to rent a two-story grey beach house in an Italian neighborhood in East Haven that had porches on both floors and a concrete deck that jutted out to the edge of the water. 176R Cosey Beach Avenue. I recall committing that address to memory as part of a third-grade classroom exercise.

I've lived in better neighborhoods. One neighbor, a buxom elderly woman, liked to sit on the beach in the mornings and sunbathe topless, and the neighbor on the other side, Mr. Tellerico, was a reputed Mafia don who kept killer dogs. I remember well the day my brother brought home a hypodermic syringe from the city park next door. But the place was just what Mom wanted. I remember listening to her giggle into the phone about it. "Our back yard is Long Island Sound, for God's sake," she would squeal to friends. At high tide she was absolutely right.

Mom inherited a little money just before our move following the death of a childless aunt and earmarked it for cultural events we would have missed in Martin. We took trips to Mystic Seaport, the planetarium at Bridgeport, Sturbridge Village in Massachusetts, and another one to a ski lodge at Bromley Mountain in Vermont in the fall to celebrate my little sister's birthday. We children had never seen New England foliage. During Christmas break, the whole family took a train into New York City for several days, a trip that included a Rockettes show.

Our lives at school were better as well. We attended Momauguin Elementary School just across a large parking lot from the beach house, one of nine elementary schools in the city. Personally, I was happy just for the break from my reputation, and happy to escape the Anglo names of the students in my Martin classes. Among the musical surnames at Momauguin School—Rucco, Bisi, Ferraro, Armeri, Arteiri, Limicelli, Fuguenick, Cousea, and Costanzo—Cowser, though not musical, no longer felt quite so odd. My sister's flamboyant fifth-grade teacher, Arthur Braun, even brought me in to his weakest math group to show them that a third-grader could do the work he was asking of them.

After school on Wednesdays, Mom drove my sisters to Branford for Irish step dancing lessons and stitched their intricate performance costumes while she waited outside in the car. Jimmy and I lacked the discipline for lessons of any kind, but we were more than content to take our plastic beach pails to the rocks along the beach behind the house, checking tide pools for rock crabs, which we caught by the back of the shell and carried home. When they died, suffocated in our pails, my brother dried them on the first-floor porch so that he and his friends could use them as smelly spaceships. Failing to find crabs, say at high-tide time, Jimmy and I bothered fishermen on the seawall to see their catch, and failing even that, asked to see their bait.

I'm not sure if my mother was really happier in East Haven or not. She knew the whole arrangement was only temporary: at the end of nine months, we'd have to go back to Martin. And as the end of our hiatus approached, my mother pleaded with my father to find a means of staying, though there really was little room for debate. I remember her sitting on the screened second-floor porch one of the last nights, after the cause had been lost, holding a drink in her hand and watching the lights of ships on the Sound and the lights of New York beyond them, talking to me about going back to Tennessee as though I were much older than I was, as though I could understand or help. "The last thing you children need is to go back to that place," she told me.

My dad drove the family Gran Torino wagon home, but the rest of us flew to Nashville and arrived ahead of him. We found that the members of the college rodeo team to whom we had rented the Tennessee house had wrecked the place: tracked manure from their boots on every carpet in the house, cleaned a bird on the floor in one of the bedrooms, stolen an heirloom rug of my father's. That didn't help the transition. My mother cried until Dad arrived several days later.

Upon returning to Martin, my siblings and I more or less assumed the positions in Martin society that we had occupied before leaving. But we were changed. I expect my mother knew the trip would be just that way, formative, like a summer at a lake cabin or in Europe. One of the things you learn growing up in a place like Martin is to seize upon times like that, to make little movies of such moments in your head, later to screen them in your mind's eye as you lie in bed at night during periods of lesser stimulation. Maybe Mom had been living that way a long time herself. We kids began planning our escapes from Martin right there on Cosey Beach Avenue, plotting our way back to that place or one like it.

Things changed for my parents too. The tense embrace they shared at our back door once my dad got home, a plastic bag under his arm full of souvenirs from a night he spent somewhere in Virginia, was their last public display of affection for quite a long time. They remain stubbornly married today, having somehow survived a bizarre period in the early eighties when it seemed the parents of almost every university kid I knew were getting divorced. So many mothers had abandoned degrees and careers to raise their families full-time and later were thinking better of it. I almost always believe we kids were better off for our parents staying together, but I have to wonder about my parents.

I know my mother had thought about leaving, something she talked with me about the summer both my brother and I were divorcing our first wives, as though she envied us a little. Jimmy often reminds me of the several times Mom packed a small children's suitcase with a nightgown, a hairbrush, and a carton of cigarettes and moved into the Len Haven Motel for three or four nights, coming back when she just couldn't stand being away from us one minute longer. What life could she, a marginally employed mother of four kids, have made for herself in that place without my father anyway? It wasn't a risk she was willing to take.

Dad left too. I went with him once to a little room in the Martin Plaza Motel and spent what seemed like the loneliest night of my life there. Had I clung to his leg fearing he'd leave for good, or was I scared to stay behind? Maybe I just wanted the novelty of a night in a motel. Then for the whole summer following our time in Connecticut, Dad lived three hours away in Nashville working as an editor for a small religious publisher—it's where he got started writing poetry. Mom drove all of us kids over to see him one weekend, to visit Opryland and sleep on the floor of his one-bedroom apartment, but it never occurred to me that he might not come home.

Returning home to Canton, New York, from a trip to Massachusetts a few years ago, I insisted on making a sixty-mile detour to East Haven to see the old house on Cosey Beach Avenue. I found the spot with no trouble, by memory, but the house hardly resembled the one we'd lived in. We drove to Momauguin School too, where I found my third-grade classroom.

It's probably not that unusual to return to the homes of your childhood like they were historical sites or the scenes of some unsolved crime. Phillip Lopate says family is a puzzle never solved. It's just that there's rarely enough evidence there to make real determinations about what happened.

I certainly thought I was saying to hell with Martin when I left for college almost twenty years ago. Though it made growing up there difficult, I have mostly enjoyed the grudge I have imagined exists between me and that place. It has been a supreme motivation, offering me, time and again, a kind of traction to get myself out of ruts and rough patches. But I am learning of late that it is foolish to insist on hating your hometown. George Orwell cautions those of us who would write about our childhoods that we must beware of exaggeration and self-pity, distorted as every child's vision of the world is. The need I have always felt to settle scores with people there has given way to a more pressing need to really belong to some place, which I understand now can really only be Martin.

I could never really wring that place out of my laundry anyway. I learned this from my father, who has moved all over the country and yet has never managed to leave the dirt farm in rural East Texas on which he was raised, taking it with him everywhere he goes, the red dirt caked in the furrows between his toes and against his inner ankle under his socks. You can only come from one place, and it sticks with you, good and bad.

In spite of my stubborn wish to do it, I was never really able to hate Martin entirely, though I feel oddly disloyal to my mother in this. I admit

I am aghast when things from the old days in Martin pass into oblivion, even if they are things or people I once eyed with loathing or derision—The Ticklebone Bar-B-Q, Pacer Pete's Puttin' Place, Jo's Antique Mall and Hairstyling Mart, the musty Varsity Theater. I feel compelled to enumerate them all here lest any one of them end up on the garbage heap of history. Even I know what a shame that would be.

# Wild Begins Here

**B**enjamin Gilmer was the first to spot it, a full foot long and the color of mud, moving slowly in the stagnant fountain water. The afternoon we finished our sixth-grade final exams, a couple of school friends and I had pedaled our bikes to the Virginia Weldon Park and found swimming in the old fountain there a full-grown carp. Mike Hopper called it a carp anyway, though none of us were sure of the fish's taxonomy.

Martin Junior High held only half-days of class during exam week, so one night while studying together for a history test in Benjamin's bedroom, Benjamin reclining on his waterbed and Mike and I cross-legged on the floor, the three of us had agreed to ride our bikes the two miles to school the next day instead of taking the bus. We had ceased to look at bike-riding as something to be done for its own sake, and our bikes had fallen out of fashion and into disrepair. Mine was a blue Schwinn hand-me-down, a banana-seated rattletrap adorned with decals left over from my model airplanes. Still, bikes allowed my friends and me to take full advantage of the liberty of the half-day off from school, and to do it with some dignity. It was simply uncool to ride the bus or, worse yet, take rides from your parents. We were too young, the three of us, to know much yet about what we wanted from our lives, aside from our collective wish to be local sports heroes some years down the road, so we mostly bowed to our parents' wishes and plans: they urged us to study hard, take music or art lessons, work after-school jobs, better ourselves in general. By and large we did not depart from those dicta. We were not adventurous in any real way. At times, though, like this particular afternoon, when we found a crack in the long, white fence of days, we managed to squeeze ourselves through.

When classes let out at noon that day, the three of us walked our bikes in the noon-bright sun across the railroad tracks behind the school's gymnasium to busy Lindell Street. Once we reached Lindell, we mounted the bikes and rode toward downtown, stopping halfway in to pick up burgers at the Sonic drive-in. We continued downtown and pedaled past the storefronts—Otasco, the American Café, Ben Franklin's —then coasted behind the post office and the electric company to the

*Ben Franklin Department Store, Lindell Street, on a rare snowy day, Martin, Tenn., circa 1980. Photograph courtesy of the Special Collections and Archives, University of Tennessee at Martin. Used by permission*

park. Rectangular in shape and the size of a large backyard, the city park was distinguished from other lots only by wooden park benches and the century-old oak trees that lined and shaded the property. The fountain lay at its heart.

Almost as soon as we spotted the fish, Mike had volunteered to ride to his house, less than a mile away on McGill Street, to get his fishing net. Benjamin and I decided to stay behind and keep an eye on the fish. Our fish was not pretty. *Macabre* was a better word. His large scales were the size of our fingertips, larger even, and he bore whiskers at his snout. But we thought our fish wonderfully monstrous, gliding over the layers of coins on the fountain floor.

Leaning on our elbows on the fountain's edge, a lip of white concrete rich with moss and bird droppings, neither Benjamin nor I could resist the temptation to stick our hands into the three feet of filthy water and reach for the carp. The fountain went unused most of the year, and knowing as little about fountains as we did, we were not at all sure we wouldn't be soaked should it come suddenly to life. Of course, the fish darted from our hands even as they broke the water's surface. When Mike returned to the park with the net a few minutes later, the fish became even cagier, propelling himself backward and backward, using his pectoral fins like small oars, winding himself away from Mike's clumsy net pole and toward the intricate web of pipes and nozzles at the center of the dormant fountain.

"Do you think it grew up in there somehow?" Benjamin asked.

"You mean from when it was a baby," Mike shot back, taking his turn with his hand in the soupy, lukewarm water. "Not likely." This was the way it usually went: Mike was brash, the recognized authority on everything. His father taught science at our junior high. Benjamin was naively inquisitive. I was always somewhere else in my head. I was thinking in that moment of a favorite childhood book of mine, *The Fast-Talking Dolphin,* the story of a boy who finds a talking saltwater dolphin living in a pond behind his house and builds a salt grinder to keep the dolphin alive. How wonderful it would have been to keep our carp alive there, to visit him daily, feed him—secretly, of course.

We could not explain how the fish got there, nor did we feel a compelling need to do so. We received such curiosities like small sacraments, secular weekday counterparts to the Sunday miracles we accepted on faith. We received that fish as we received the other ordinary miracles of our lives: the love of our parents, the safety of our homes. In those years we sought the sense of things only half-urgently, and failing to find this sense hardly troubled us. How the fish came to be there in the fountain we could not say, and whether the fish was in fact a carp none of us could be certain. We were content to wonder.

Mike's pole soon scraped up so much grime and algae from the bottom of the fountain that we lost sight of the fish in the cloudy water. After a few fruitless attempts at collecting the change from the bottom of the fountain with Mike's net, we agreed to move on and return to the park the next day to check on the fish. Then we rode our bikes home, each boy his own way.

I could not keep our secret, even overnight. Still, I was quietly proud that I had told only my brother and my parents about the fish once I got home. But when Mike, Benjamin, and I returned on foot to the fountain the following morning, the carp had disappeared. I can recall now summer evenings when my brother and two sisters and I were very young children and my parents watched us chase fireflies gleefully around our backyard, helped us catch them in our fat fists and place them in mayonnaise jars. Though Mom and Dad poked thin holes in the jar lids with butter knives so our lightning bugs could breathe, we always woke the next day to empty jars and the kind of inner emptiness I felt that morning about the fountain carp.

I said nothing of my sense of loss to Benjamin or Mike. We had active friendships, as I say, friendships based on rivalry and roughhousing and one-upmanship—as opposed, I guess, to the contemplative friendships I formed more selectively later in my life. Perhaps we were a bit suspicious too, about who'd finked about the carp, who'd come back later and taken it for himself. In a matter of a few days, we had moved on to Babe Ruth league baseball and summer lawn-mowing jobs, and we were never really friends after sixth grade.

The fish in the fountain was probably the drunk prank of local men or boys on their way home from a day of fishing at one of the many rivers, lakes, or fishing holes around our hometown. I see that now. Martin lies within an hour's drive of Reelfoot Lake, the Mississippi, Tennessee, and Obion Rivers, and the Land between the Lakes in Kentucky. I can imagine the thunder of the truck mufflers as the fishermen pull into the park, their hoots as they hoist the huge fish into the fountain. Perhaps they climb in themselves and splash around with the day's catch. Maybe they come back for him the next night, drunk again, collect him, cut him up, and eat him. I could not have imagined such a thing when I was twelve, but I can picture it clearly now.

The truest comforts of a rural Tennessee childhood like mine were the perceptible edges to things, edges to what you know and don't. During the two years I lived in Milwaukee as a graduate student, I was greatly unsettled by the fact that I could not find the edge of town. If I kept traveling south, Milwaukee seemed to become Chicago somewhere along the way, imperceptibly. Where one city ended, the other began. There had been clear lines drawn between Martin and surrounding communities—Latham, Sidonia, Palmersville, Hornbeak—and city limits had meant something. They meant "wild begins here." Drive to the edge of any small town like Martin and find a city limit sign. Notice how the paved city street ends at that point, how the road beyond, maintained by the county, becomes red clay and gravel just where the sign is staked in the ground. Take that city limit marker at high speed in your car and see if you don't feel wilder by degrees as the car leaves town and your tires begin to churn the clay to dust. Follow the county road out a ways, notice how it leaves the rigorous grid of the city streets and hugs the natural bend and curve of the land. Things, even roads, go wild past the city limits. But within those limits, a boy could expect civility, order. Seeing the transgressing fish there captivated us the way seeing a worn centerfold might have. We were boys on the edge of summer, and the hard edges to things were just beginning to feel like restraints.

Despite this auspicious beginning as a naturalist, I am a bit ashamed to say I grew up just another "great indoorsman." I went on to watch a lot of cable television and swim in indoor, chlorinated pools. I was not a Boy Scout for long, nor was I a hunter or a fisherman, as my friend Mike Hopper was. In fact, my family will balk at my writing of the natural world at all. Maybe the fact that my parents were town-dwelling college teachers and not farmers or park rangers prevented me from becoming wholly a part of any natural place. My father can take a walk seemingly anywhere he finds himself and begin to name for me indigenous flora and fauna as he encounters them: lespedeza, cicada, Indian paintbrushes, the grey dove. But I am lost in such a situation.

This environmentally conscious generation of students I now find myself teaching is making a difference, as is my young son Jackson, who is full of wonder and curiosity about the creatures that inhabit our northern New York backyard (I have to say I prefer Jackson's wonder). A few winters back, during a cold snap that saw the mercury fall below zero night and day for nearly two solid weeks, the smaller rodents of our neighborhood started finding ways into our very old house, where it was warm. Common rodents mostly, mice and squirrels. My wife and I heard them crawling in the walls late at night, found their teeth marks in our bars of bath soap and their droppings on the piles of folded towels in our bathroom closets. The evening a squirrel appeared atop our microwave, we decided we'd had enough and called in animal control. A squirrel wrangler set some traps, baited with peanut butter, near the places where he thought the larger animals might be getting in, gaps between our home's vinyl siding and its original façade. Sure enough, the next morning we woke to find squirrels in five of the six traps.

But it was the sixth trap that was most interesting. Inside we found an honest-to-God ermine, of "The Lady Is a Tramp" fame, more commonly known, Jackson and I learned on the Internet that night, as the white weasel. We read that ermine were very fierce, like wolverines, and that Ontario and northern New York represented the southernmost area of what was an otherwise polar range. I had noticed that while the frantic squirrels had bloodied themselves trying to get out of the traps, the ermine was a cool customer, biding his time before the pounce. The animal control officer asked to take the ermine home so he could put him to work catching mice and rats in his barn but told us later the weasel was gone within a day.

I think of the caged ermine often these days. Watching him for that short time outside our home, watching my son watch him and then helping the boy learn all he could about the animal, I thought of myself as a boy and my souvenir fish and how far I'd gotten from home.

# One Good Barbecue
# Sandwich Away

**M**y parents continue to send me news clippings from the *Weakley County Press* to remind me where I come from. They mail the clippings by the handful, mostly the wedding announcements of my old classmates or the write-ups of Westview Charger football victories, folding each story's dateline to the width of its one or two columns and then stuffing all the stories in an envelope. The news is not always good, of course, and though I promised my parents that as long as they lived in Martin I would refrain from writing letters to the editor of the *Press,* I am tempted to do it now and then. One story in particular has been troubling me.

I gather from the news clippings that during a debate about school consolidation, the chairwoman of the local school board told her fellow board members that rural life in the South was dead and that they needed to face facts and move on. The old boys took it badly. Many objected to her remark in the write-up of the meeting that appeared on the front page of the paper. Their friends wrote letters to the editor. My parents say that soon after that board meeting, the pretty checkers at the Big Star grocery were telling about the threats made against the

*The American Café, Lindell Street, Martin, Tenn., circa 1965. Photograph courtesy of the Special Collections and Archives, University of Tennessee at Martin. Used by permission*

Indiana-born chairwoman's life, the flak vest she was now wearing to board meetings at the insistence of the county sheriff. Some people said it made you proud to be a Tennessean and a Christian to hear the old men talk about "way of life" again. But me, I thought it was silly. The old boys needed no one to tell them that the world as they knew it was on its final spin. There were signs enough.

Perhaps there is nothing more emblematic of the wane of what was best in the Old South than the all-but-unheralded passing of the American Café's "Barbecue Plate." Though Martin has never been any more than a late-night stop on the Illinois Central Gulf line, at least the South still had its home-baked goodness when my parents moved us there thirty-five years ago. This was when a barbecue sandwich, sweet and tangy and thick in your mouth, might still be had at the American Café on Lindell Street, served with a side of creamy slaw, a sealed package of saltines, and a toothpick, when a half-dozen clown cookies or gingerbread men might still be gotten next door at the Martin Bakery with your morning cup, when filling station restrooms all over town were rich in their filth and oily brownness and the afternoon sun and the pure belly-dream of barbecue still drew the old men of the Parkview Hotel out into the shade of the century oaks to have a tangy sandwich to go.

But this New South heralded in all the magazines has meant nothing to the people of Martin, Tennessee, if it has not meant compromise and loss. The late Willie Morris wrote that if modern industrialism and the American urge to homogeneity came later to his native Mississippi, it also arrived with greater destructiveness. Too many daddies left the farm to build tires all night out at Goodyear in Union City, and too many mommas went to work second jobs at night while the daddies were gone, fixing vacuum cleaners or renting videos or watching someone else's children, so that no one had time to stop by the café anymore. It closed down rather quietly several years ago. Gone are the sandwiches and squarish formica tables they were served on, the old men in feed hats and coveralls who gathered there, and the Kiwanis gum ball machines that sat on the sidewalk out front. Jo's Antique Furniture Mall and Hairstyling Mart has taken the café's place downtown on Lindell, and the Video and Yogurt Outlet has replaced the Martin Bakery. First somebody made a church out of the old Varsity Theater, of all things, then a sports rehab clinic. British Petroleum has bought up the filling stations around town and cleaned up the bathrooms. They are "service stations" now.

Out at the McDonald's on the bypass, I can find the café's old lunch crowd if I am looking hard. They seem somewhat bewildered by the sandwiches of the new order, wrapped in wax paper and stuffed in styrofoam boxes, and the talk has dried up. The ritual of the café's plate lunch has been replaced, in the years since I left, by the hollow rite of the drive-thru McRib. If you take away a person's lunch, I submit to you there is little left.

All this has been especially sad for my family, since our move to Martin was to be, for our father at least, a return. And if Dad had left the South fleeing what was bad those years ago (and you don't need to

*The author's father, Dr. Robert G. Cowser, in his office in the Humanities Building at the University of Tennessee at Martin, circa 1985. The painting visible on the wall behind his head is the work of his brother R. L. From the author's family collection*

tell me about what was bad), he had returned for what was good, what he missed—brown bathrooms and pulled-pork sandwiches, the stringier the better.

Since the closing of the café, Dad lunches mostly at home, mostly by himself. Perhaps he has a stack of Ritz crackers, one or two carrot sticks from his dish of water in the fridge, maybe on a banner day a celery stalk, its gullet full of peanut butter, or a Fig Newton. He rests them on a tiny saucer just so and sits down with his glass of iced tea.

But as he gives a bit of carrot its thirty-two chews, isn't he thinking of the sandwich of the old regime? Perhaps he is still thinking of the ghostly sandwich once he gets back to the office, the way you dream about dinner all day long some days, until something interrupts him: a knock at his door or a phone call. It is not so strange, after all, to love a sandwich that way. I knew a girl in college from Chicago who had a Reuben sandwich every time she saw it on the menu and said she was searching for the world's best and some day would write a book about it. "Sometimes I wonder if your poor father isn't one good old-fashioned barbecue sandwich away from being truly happy," my mother once told me on the phone.

Now and again, when Dad drives my brother or sister or me to the airport in Memphis, we indulge him with a visit to the Longtown Restaurant just off Interstate 55 in Somerville. The restaurant itself is nothing to speak of, really only the dark back corner of a service station quick stop, separated from the service station by racks of potato

*The author's father and uncle R. L. Cowser on the running board of their sister Juanita's car, 1940. From the author's family collection*

*R. L. Cowser aboard a Russian merchant ship bound for Alexandria, summer 1987. From the author's family collection*

*R. L. Cowser and the author's father, circa 1938. From the author's family collection*

*R. L. Cowser and the author's father, circa 1938. From the author's family collection*

chips and snack cakes. But back there in the dark, behind the potato chips and the cold drink coolers, they serve the contraband sandwich as you like it, open face or whatever, and the waitresses in their short, pink getups call Dad and me "boys" though my father is now past seventy. "What can I get you boys?" one of the ladies might say to us, or, to my father, "More tea, honey?" They serve good iced tea as well at the Longtown, which is itself no longer an automatic, even that close to Memphis. That place is still what Martin was once all about. I wish I could tell you about Dad's face when he eats one of those sandwiches.

Often when I'm away and Dad passes through Somerville on his way somewhere else, maybe to Memphis to get a shot for his wasp-sting allergy, he sends me a postcard from the Longtown. "Had a Sandwich," he writes on the back. Nothing else. On the front of the card, perhaps there is a likeness of Elvis, or a photo of the Memphis skyline, or of the Smoky Mountains. But I always think how there should be a photo of the sandwich on that card, messy and big and fat as a man's fist.

# The Heart Is a
# Dark Forest

S ince high school, I have held a certain picture in my mind—by
force of will. In the foreground kids stand before a restored
Model T in poses of adolescent bravado or coquetry, guys with porkpie
hats and tommyguns and girls in long strands of faux pearls and flapper
dresses. Behind them rows of milo run vertically to the bright horizon.
A conspicuously small boy rides the running board of the Model T in a
pinstripe suit and a hat that he has cocked over one eye, his dark locks
spilling from under its brim, the trace of a fine, boyish mustache shad-
ing his lip.

My image is stenciled from the real, from the black and white student council photograph in my senior yearbook, snapped in a field out
behind our high school during the week before school started in August.
The boy on the running board is my best childhood friend, Kip Estlin.
I have always thought how the picture captured him—his trademark
live fast, exquisite corpse routine. Though it was a grainy print, ama-
teurish, I tell myself I can make out in his eyes the alluring specter of
sedition.

But Susan Sontag says the lie of a photograph is the false promise
of any graven image: this claim to possession of anything very real or

essential about what we cherish. Photographs preserve nothing but traces of light. And there are dark things about us and those we love we cannot remove with wishing. It was after I had been gone from Martin a handful of years, when I heard Kip's name thrown around in discussions of the mysterious death of a local girl, that the photograph became for me a haunted thing.

As a child, I equated Kip's look of sedition and mischief with genius. I should say here that I define genius rather broadly. For me there is deliberate genius, the sort that allows a man like Handel to compose mind-blowing music in a one-room house full of noisy children, the kind we lionize for its gifts to posterity. And then there is reckless genius, the genius that seems to walk holding beauty by one hand and danger by the other. Think James Dean and Steve McQueen. It destroys, I'm afraid, more than it produces, and has little mind for posterity. That was Kip's kind. I remember that he was a bold and imaginative talker and that I found myself preferring lies he told to the official versions of the truth.

Neither Kip nor I were born in Martin, and since that matters a great deal to folks who were, we found ourselves thrown together as young boys. Our parents worked together at the local college, so he and I grew up side by side doing the kinds of things every boy does, presuming as we did them in what we thought was a manner beyond the imaginations of other kids we knew, something important to us. This was the cold war's height, and I remember we killed a lot of imaginary Russkies and various other commies in the fields behind his house. In quieter moments we designed and named new Air Force fighter jets, collaborating on highly detailed cutaway drawings, sure to place our names just below the cockpit canopies, taking turns as pilot and rear gunner. I don't recall that we ever quarreled. We seemed to sense how important the friendship was.

Part of Kip's genius was extravagance. He once invited me over to watch a meteor shower, and we stayed up all night, washing a full box of Hostess cupcakes down with a liter of grape soda. At the movies Kip would buy five or six candy bars and shove them into his giant tub of buttered popcorn, then we would lose ourselves in the old Varsity Theater, as you are given to do at the movies when you are eight or nine. The Varsity owned only one LP in those days, Journey's *Escape*. Always early for the feature, we draped our legs over the back of the seats in front of us and listened endlessly to "Who's Crying Now" and "Stone in Love."

Somehow everything changed when we stepped out of the Varsity into the world again, though. Trouble always found us. Even as a child, Kip did not appreciate the provincialism of Martin authority, nor it him. Suffice it to say, my idea that he was a genius was not shared by the boys who were our peers, "townies" who stayed at home for college and are now semirespectable accountants and policemen and junior high football coaches and will in ten years be county commissioners and aldermen and church elders. They reserved a special hatred for my friend. And though Kip never grew to be any taller than 5'2" or so, hardly weighing more than one hundred pounds the whole time I knew him, he was fierce when it came to a fight and better than anyone I've ever met at picking one. I was always there to fight the fights he picked too. I did it gladly because I understood that he knew more about the world I wanted to live in than any of the teachers or parents I knew. I now think fighting beside him was my way of saying that. We became the best argument the local school board had for the widespread administration of Ritalin to schoolboys, kicked out of schools, soccer games, skating rinks, scout troops, and swimming pools, mostly for fighting with other boys who, truth be told, had asked for it. For many years that distinction only made us closer. There is no loyalty like that we know as children.

At some point, though, I began to wonder why we did all that carousing, realized that maybe I'd never known, and while Kip never got much bigger, the stakes that accompanied associating with him did. I guess I was ultimately a chickenshit when it came to doing what I needed to do to keep pace with him. I just wanted things to go easier for me. I wanted less trouble, which I realize now is probably a very cowardly thing.

Once while the two of us were attending a Presbyterian church camp a hundred miles from home, I walked into the cabin Kip and I shared to find him locked up in a fight with another camper, a minister's boy from Trenton, digging furrows in the skin of the poor boy's neck with his fingernails. The Trenton boy was swinging wildly but connecting with nothing. Though he didn't seem to need it, I came to Kip's aid just as our counselor broke up the fight. Afterward I was embarrassed. I had been quietly enjoying myself at the camp, and I realized, sitting in the camp director's office hours later, listening to the drone of his voice and the whine of a ceiling fan under it, that I didn't want to be a part of it anymore. That was a new feeling.

Things changed further after Kip's parents' unseemly divorce during my eighth grade year—his father was of the opinion that perhaps I was influencing Kip's misbehavior in school and elsewhere and discouraged our hanging around. I did attend the birthday party Kip threw himself the following year while his father was in Japan on business, with only his twenty-something Japanese stepmother there to supervise. It was great fun until drunken Kip passed out behind a locked bathroom door upstairs and the rest of us panicked and called in our parents. After that I hardly saw him, just here and there around high school. I played football, but Kip needed none of that rah-rah stuff. He was into anything experimental and avant-garde, and in Martin that limited him to college parties, garage bands, beer, and drugs. Somewhere else he might have been someone else, but that is the point of all of this.

I tried to convince myself that all of this losing touch was natural. Yet whenever Kip did find me, in the halls or at ball games or whatever, he acted as though our being apart for so long were some sort of misunderstanding, as though I just didn't know that we went to the same school. That always made me feel hollow. I remember the first time I saw that yearbook photograph having the troubling feeling that there was no place for me in the picture, and I could not have told you why. Even now.

I cannot say, either, that I was surprised when I heard midway through my sophomore year of college that Kip had finally gotten himself into serious trouble. My mother wrote to tell me Kip had been named in a civil wrongful death suit involving the death of a young girl the year before in what had first been determined an ATV accident. My mother included an article from the *Press* with the few available details. "I feel so much for poor Joy Estlin," my mother wrote in her letter. Joy was Kip's mother, a bright woman from Minnesota who had divorced Kip's father and inexplicably lost the boys in a custody battle. At the time of the girl's death, she was living alone in Boston, always behind dark glasses, trying to finish a Northeastern Ph.D. she'd abandoned to start her family years before.

Kip's trouble was serious indeed. According to the lawsuit filed by the dead girl's parents, there had been no three-wheeler accident. The plaintiffs contend, in fact, that the seventeen-year-old son of a prominent local physician had actually beaten the girl to death with a dining-room chair during a party at the doctor's home. In his panic the doctor's boy had convinced the county coroner, a longtime family friend, to stage the girl's death as an accident, thus preventing a criminal investigation. Kip was named in the suit because he was a friend of the doctor's boy and had attended the party, which he admitted later had gotten out of hand. Since the suit had been filed, the state had taken over the civil case. The paper reported that while investigators had not exhumed the body to that point, they would if the need arose in order to prove, as those who saw her body contend, that her head had been crushed unnaturally, that her injuries were not indicative of any accident, of anything but rage.

Maybe three months after reading about his trouble, I finally saw Kip —a blue December dusk. It does not get very cold in the soybean delta, but it does get dark. I was home from college in New Orleans and was running on the fitness trail the university had constructed west of the campus. I could see the lights of the Wal-Mart parking lot just over the top of the small grove of trees at the westernmost end of the winding trail as I ran, and I could see myself very sharply in the still pond at the center of the trail.

Then I saw Kip, or his reflection, running up the trail from behind me, as if out of my past. It was not only his height that remembered him to me but his gait as well, which was the same gait that had carried him across the soccer field as a child and around the skating rink years ago. I think I would have liked to disappear just then, to slip into whatever part of the twilight Kip had appeared from, and I am ashamed to say that. But it would have made things simpler for me. I slowed down until I thought he could see who I was through the night. When he caught up, he could not have been more excited to see me, or more pleased about all the things he'd heard about my life in New Orleans.

I learned that though he'd graduated one summer later than the rest of his class, he'd earned a National Merit Scholarship to attend the University of Oregon. He loved the West, he said, and he wanted to tell me all about it over a few beers. "Sure, call me," I said.

"He'll never call," I promised my parents, who were very sure for understandable reasons that I shouldn't see Kip. Something in me said I should go, something louder said he wouldn't call. And when the phone rang a few hours later, I did not jump or anything like that. This is not a horror story. It could have been anybody, after all. My sisters and brother and I were all home, and the phone never stops ringing when that is the case. Even when my little brother stepped into my room to tell me the phone was for me, I did not think much about who it was.

But as I walked across the family room and saw my mother in the doorway of the kitchen, I knew the phone was Kip. She held him far from her body and did not look at me. I stepped into the kitchen and took the phone from her as she moved away.

"Hey, Bobby," the voice on the phone said, "thiz Kip." He had always slurred those words together.

"Hey," I said.

"Up for Cadillacs tonight?" the voice said. All of our hairbreadth escapes and tiny childhood insurrections seemed to return in that moment to stand between us in those phone lines.

My mother was stirring something on the stove and not looking at me and pretending not to eavesdrop, and the long fluorescent bulb over the stove was so bright that I could not see out into the night, though I looked very intently through the window.

"Nine o'clock?" I said.

My mother's shoulders fell.

"See you there," said the voice.

It should have felt better to do it, I guess, to stand beside him again after all that time. I walked across the house to shower. When I walked out of the house into the night sometime later, I found my mother sitting in the carport, smoking. There were no other lights on in that end of the house, so that the only light I could see was the burning end of her cigarette, glowing brighter with each deep breath she took. I could not see her, and I could not see if she saw me. If she could see me standing there in the night, she might have known that I stood there a long time trying to tell her why I was going, that I was standing there a long time trying to tell her all those things you want to tell your mother but never seem to. I walked to the car.

Cadillacs was a hole-in-the-wall bar on Church Street in downtown Martin. "Downtown" was in its heyday a strip only four or five blocks and one traffic light long, but it had by this time been undone by the Wal-Mart and accompanying franchises built out near the Highway 45 Bypass. In fact, Cadillacs may have been the only profitable business venture in that area of town at the time, one door teeming with bodies amid a score of empty and abandoned buildings. Cadillacs served beer, after all, and in a "dry" county that was all it took to make the place something of an oasis.

I met Kip in the parking lot there. The bar itself was dimly lit. Only the rectangular lamps that hung a few feet above the pool tables illuminated the place—much as street lamps do the sidewalk—dividing it up, leaving whole pockets of the room dark, so that I could hardly make out who was there. Kip walked to an empty table. I couldn't have cared less about playing pool, to be honest. He put down our quarters and racked the balls.

After some time, faces began to lean in from the darkness to look at us playing, and I began to recognize the men and boys as many we had tangled with before—at church camp, perhaps, in school, at the skating rink, on the soccer field. They were leaning in to the light of the pool table lamps so that we could see them and they could see us and we'd all know the score—that they finally had Kip where they'd wanted him. They all read the paper, and whether any of it was true mattered little to them.

Kip and I stood there in that bar drinking beer a long time: him looking at me, then his beer; me doing the same. It is an awful thing to be stared at. Kip must have been waiting for me to suggest we leave, because I was waiting for him. At long last, around midnight, when he was sure he'd annoyed the regulars, I suppose, Kip suggested we buy more beer and gas at a convenience store before they all closed and cruise town. I agreed quickly.

He drove a few blocks to a convenience store, where we each bought a six-pack of beer and I bought a handful of red-hot Color Bubbles gum balls, because I hated the taste of beer in those days and hated more to tell him. He pulled from the parking lot and drove immediately out of town, west toward Union City and the Mississippi.

It was a good idea to get out of town. From almost any point in the neighborhood where I grew up—not only from points of the slightest elevation, like the little crown in the pavement where McGill Street becomes Clearwater, but on clear days even from the edge of the swift creek below Redbud Circle that winds along the city limit—a boy could see the steeples of the churches downtown. But once you drive out of the Martin city limits, out to the bypass and beyond, where before you realize it the paved highway becomes gravel back road and you are as likely to see a deer as another car, it is as though you have broken free of whatever grip that place has on you and you are beyond all the glaring and everything else, and you can think a thought all the way out, watch it fall from the edge of the delta like a marble rolling off the edge of some strange table. Out there it is as though you could drive back to the time no one in Martin spoke of within the hearing of ministers, the time before the shadows of men and women and steeples darkened creek bottoms, the time before stories even. It was just Kip and me under a sky full of stars—old times.

We were not talking, just drinking. Kip finally spoke, somewhere between Martin and Union City on a new stretch of highway. I had never been out there before. It was barely lit and all but deserted.

"Wasn't all that stuff in Henry County wild?" he said. Henry County was the next county over, where the girl was killed.

"Yeah," I said.

He paused as if he were deciding whether he needed to say what came next.

"I had nothing to do with it, you know," he said.

"I know," I said.

He didn't say any more, only drove. But it was an easy, comfortable silence again, like before. On a stretch of the new highway just outside of Union City, I felt him slow the car down and pull off to the side of the road on a narrow shoulder. "Gotta take a leak," Kip half shouted, and he turned off the lights and climbed out of the car.

I was drunk by now. There were no lights out there, so the sky was so dark I could see the real color of the night, which if you look at it is not black at all but a rich, bruised blue. I heard the cold water of the North Fork of the Obion River running along the new highway and heard Kip open the trunk and begin to rummage around, then close the trunk and move to the side of the road to pee. I thought in that moment of a story I'd heard about Butch Cassidy and the Sundance Kid—how the two had fled the law to Bolivia a hundred years ago, and how one (no one is sure which) shot the other and then turned the gun on himself, and how the two were buried in unmarked graves lost to us now. I had a thought of the dead girl. I thought of how much I was like Kip, yet how I would never truly be like Kip because I was chicken.

Then he was back in the car. "I got the rest of the beer," he said. "Good," I said, and I took the last gum ball I had and shoved it in my mouth.

# Good Turns

*For Ted*

**A**t the end of my freshman year at Loyola University in uptown New Orleans, my Biever Hall resident assistant, John Barrett, recommended me to the directors of Residential Life for a tutoring program they were establishing on the top floor of the twelve-story women's dorm. The directors had announced that they were seeking strong students to fill the rooms on the top floor of Buddig Hall and needed the help of the resident assistants in culling candidates from the pool of students who already lived in the dorms.

At the time, I thought of John's favor in the only way I knew how: I supposed John was pulling strings just to get me into the girls' dorm. Fine with me, I thought—I had read in my sister's *Cosmopolitan* that the key element in any romance was proximity. Loyola had strict visitation policies—no men in Buddig except as registered guests of female residents, no men period after midnight—so this appointment seemed like a real entrée into the building my friends called the tower of chastity. "Foxes in the henhouse," my Buddig roommate Chris Williamson used to say. So when one of the Res. Life directors phoned to offer me a spot on the floor I leapt at the chance, the chance to tell people I spent every night sleeping on top of four hundred women. Perhaps you have another idea of what heaven is, and of course you are welcome to it, but when I was eighteen this new living arrangement was mine.

It is only now that I understand John's recommendation as a good turn with long-term benefits. I think I might have gone one of two ways at that point in my life, become either an egghead or a meathead, and I like to believe John Barrett recognized this and intervened. His recommendation was his way of righting my listing ship. Four or five years older than I was and on the verge of graduation, John was the bright and good-looking son of a retired Hollywood stuntman, and I could not explain his interest in me, a Tennessee naif, beyond the fact that looking out for me was in part his job as my RA. I was thankful for the interest nonetheless and would have done anything he suggested.

Did I deserve the appointment to the tutoring floor? Probably not. I was a capable student, an idea John's appointment placed in my head for the first time in my life, though I was not extraordinary. There were many better students living in the dorms, members of Loyola's prestigious presidential scholars program. I had realized in my first year of college how desperately I wanted to learn, but I hadn't really gotten around to doing much of it yet. I certainly had no ability as a tutor. But opportunity can be like that, disguised or undeserved, like the love that puts it in your way, and it is still opportunity. You can do egghead things for meathead reasons and still have matters turn out okay.

All the time I was at Loyola, I held in the front of my head a memory of the day I arrived. It had been decided that my father would drive me the eight hours south to New Orleans that August. My father decided this, actually, without consultation, then broke it to my mother. Mom had driven Mary to school in Boston two years earlier, so my father, pleased that at least one of us planned to educate himself in the South as he had, was volunteering to make this much shorter trip.

I knew Dad had other, ulterior reasons for driving as well. Before we left, Dad reminded me several times that he had visited New Orleans as a boy. His father's brother Jim Tom Cowser left their East Texas town in the thirties to become a successful plumbing contractor in the Big Easy, and my dad's family had several times gone to see him. I imagined somber adventures, Dad and his younger brother, R. L., silent in the backseat of a family roadster, while the adults—my grandparents and my great-aunt and uncle—stood outside the car to regard the city's attractions just as silently. I had no trouble imagining these vacations since trips with my father were often like that. I would think later, standing blotto before one of the long urinal troughs in some uptown New Orleans bar, that perhaps this fine porcelain fixture had been the handiwork of great-uncle Jim Tom.

Dad planned that we would stay overnight with his long-neglected Aunt Viola in Lumberton, Mississippi, on the way down then drive the final two hours into the city the next morning. Mary was not scheduled to return to college herself until after Labor Day, so she volunteered to accompany Dad and I down Interstate 55. The visit with Viola was brief and relatively painless, though as we climbed into the car to leave, my father's aunt warned him that she'd heard of many upstanding Lumberton people who'd gone into New Orleans and never come out. I had been to New Orleans four years before on a trip with my high school French club and to Loyola specifically two years later when my parents took Mary down to see the school, so I had an idea of what I was in for.

When we pulled from Freret Street onto the Loyola campus later that morning, the place was swarming with people, new students and parents who, having settled into the dorms, were on their way to the bistros on Magazine or Tchoupitoulas for an early dinner. Later, they'd wander to the French Quarter for a hurricane at Pat O'Brien's, have pictures made at the Pat O's patio, then meet up with other parents and students they'd met in the dorm lobbies and halls. My sister had made the trip with such things in mind, I think, one last hurrah as a family. The big send-off.

But as my dad placed the last item from the car on the linoleum floor of my dorm room, a plastic laundry hamper I had purchased at Wal-Mart my last night at home, he extended himself to hug me.

"Now call your mother," he said to me matter-of-factly, "and tell her we all arrived safely and that Mary and I are heading back to Martin right away."

"We're taking the long route through Vicksburg," he said, moving toward the door, "because I get so tired of the interstate."

Then he was gone.

I mark that as the first moment of the rest of my life. You could never go by what my father said; he was a man of such few words, so you often found yourself interpreting his behavior. Though he swears even now that this was no significant gesture, I have always imagined he meant to say, "Well, son, here's your life. Welcome to it." And I guess that's what matters: what I imagine he was saying. For the first time in my life, I felt utterly responsible for myself. I went to the pay phone at the end of the hall and called my mother immediately.

"He did *what?*" she shrieked when I delivered Dad's message. I felt better knowing I had ensured a very chilly reception for Dad when he got home that evening, but my mother didn't have much more to say. She had been very quiet the morning I left home, in fact, decidedly not her ebullient self. I remember hearing from my younger brother that mom had sobbed all the way home from Boston the summer she dropped my sister off at school the first time, singing along to sentimental Top 40 songs like John Waite's "Missing You," so she may have been steeling herself against another episode like that one.

She asked about my roommate, perhaps as a means of changing the subject. His name was Greg, I told her, arrived around the same time I did, a nice enough guy, a graduate of Fairfield Prep in Connecticut. This was, Greg's father explained when we met, the boy's second try at college. Greg brought with him a pair of meat-eating aquarium fish he'd acquired in the Philippines, slept all day using his soiled laundry as bedclothes, and failed to complete even one semester at Loyola. "This place is going to kill me," he said to me in a bar on his last night in town when I asked why he was going, and I believed him.

I could hear my mother's heart sinking as I complained, so before I hung up, I told her how lush and beautiful everything was in New

Orleans, which was true, and how excited I was to be there, which I wanted to be true, all in hopes of easing *her* mind. When I think about that afternoon now, I don't know what else I would have had my mother say, or my father for that matter. Every fall I watch families move new students into dorms on the campuses where I teach, and I cannot do it without thinking how absolutely painful and absolutely necessary it all is.

The first thing I did the next day was head to the bookstore in the basement of the Danna Center to buy a daily planner. I bought a wall calendar and an alarm clock too. Ground yourself in the instruments of discipline, I thought. But I understood that the pocket date book was the real key. I remembered that in high school parents of children in academic trouble brought such date books to the teachers and asked them to write the day's assignments in them so the children wouldn't forget to do the homework. I hoped this method would work for me. The irony of the fact that I had chosen "The City That Care Forgot" in which to become a serious student was not lost on me. The one I bought was black and dimpled like a Gideon's Bible and about the size of a checkbook, and I kept in the right front pocket of my jeans or shorts at all times, snug against my thigh.

So the last day of exams that spring, I placed everything I owned on a pallet I borrowed from the Residential Life office and wheeled it from my Biever Hall room across the bright quad to my new tutor room in Buddig. I didn't have much to move—it took one trip. What I brought to college in the first place had fit into two suitcases, a footlocker, and the Wal-Mart laundry hamper.

And of course the year's textbooks. Some of them I'd sold back to the bookstore for cash, but I found in the case of many others that when push came to shove I wasn't ready to part with them. By the time I graduated from Loyola and left New Orleans, I would become attached to such a load of books that the trip back to my hometown would effectively snap the axle of the family sedan into which my mother and I had loaded my effects.

As a summer resident of Buddig 12, I was a special case. The building itself was all but shut down. Other new residents of the tutoring floor, including my roommate, Chris, went home for the summer to recuperate, work lucrative summer jobs, or both. Summer school students who chose to live in university housing were given rooms in Cabra Hall on the Law School campus, several blocks down at the intersection of St. Charles Avenue and Broadway.

With no job prospects at home in Tennessee, I had chosen to look for work in New Orleans. I lacked the entrepreneurial drive to make real money waiting tables in the French Quarter as many students did, but I was lucky enough to land a cushy position right on campus as Residential Life mail clerk, and my employers allowed me to move immediately into Buddig since I was scheduled to live there the next fall anyway. The rooms on Buddig 12 were veritable penthouses, with private baths, central air, and huge windows offering panoramic views of the city. My twelfth-floor window overlooked St. Charles Avenue, Audubon Park, and the Mississippi River beyond them. I often watched huge tankers meander down the river toward the gulf.

The work was easy. Just after eight in the morning, I walked to the university post office in the Danna Center and picked up any mail addressed to residents of Biever or Buddig Halls. All on-campus students had been required to fill out mail-forwarding cards before the end of the previous term, so once I returned to the mail room I simply found the appropriate card and rerouted all but the bulk-rate mail, which I could discard or read at my discretion. By the middle of the summer, I had memorized so many forwarding addresses that I could usually finish forwarding all the mail before 11:00 A.M. (that fall, I would baffle my friends with my knowledge of precisely where they'd spent their summers). This left me the afternoon to do anything I wished, provided my bosses thought I was still sorting mail. I began to use that time to read in the silence of the mail room.

I hadn't yet declared myself an English major, opting instead to study journalism, and certainly didn't consider myself a writer, but I did have a sense of belatedness about myself as a student. I thought I had catching up to do, a whole list of books my parents had recommended to me, titles my sisters had read a long time before: *The Sound and the Fury* and

*The Catcher in the Rye* are two I remember. Many afternoons I laughed so hard at passages from Salinger or Joseph Heller or John Kennedy Toole that my superiors from down the hall in the Res. Life office walked out to check on me.

"You okay in there?" Joy Raulerson would yell through the bank of metal mailboxes.

"Fine," I always answered, shuffling to hide the novel under a stack of magazines in case she decided to come through the door.

I usually continued reading as I walked out of the mail room at the end of the day, crossing the quad to enter my room in Buddig. Living in that tower alone was like living inside my own head. Eudora Welty writes in *One Writer's Beginnings* about reading Yeats's "The Song of Wandering Aengus" while she stood in the library stacks at the University of Wisconsin, by the light of falling snow, feeling as though she could go out into that poem the way she could go out into the snow. I felt that way as I walked out into thick summer evenings.

Today I joke about that mail clerk job being not unlike the customhouse positions secured for Hawthorne and Whitman while they struggled as writers. I wasn't writing anything then, of course, only reading, but that job did afford me the time to make forays into the contemplative life I doubt I would have afforded myself otherwise. The wonderful irony in all this, of course, is that when I think of my time in Buddig Hall, it is not the haremlike experience I dreamed about having there that I recall—more often than not the girls who came up to the twelfth floor after hours wore curlers and bathrobes and wanted only to be "friends." Instead, it is the practically monastic experience I actually had living alone those summer months that I remember. I found myself excited about the rest of my life, what became of my life after my father had dropped me off that afternoon the year before. The fresh start I'd been looking for finally presented itself, even more radically than I'd imagined. The pressure that accompanied my life during the rest of the year, self-imposed pressures to win friends and girlfriends and impress my parents, the powerful and confusing desires of adolescence, dissipated in those months. That was the power of solitude.

It was at about this time that Ted Cotton came into my life. Influenced by my summer reading, I guess, I decided once classes resumed to take on a second major in English after all, and the dean's office had directed me to Dr. Cotton, the English department's silver-bearded director of advising. His was a small corner office on the second floor of Bobet Hall overlooking the green quad, its walls adorned with Renaissance prints and photos of his wife and daughter Alice, a year or two ahead of me at Loyola.

He wore a summer-weight suit and a thin, collegiate necktie clipped to his shirt that afternoon. Small and slightly built, he struck me as formal in manner, speech, and dress, a bit on the finicky, fastidious side. Yet I sensed his warm and gentle spirit too, and he had a nasally titter that I liked immediately.

"Whom have you studied with in journalism?" Ted asked me, looking over my transcripts. I told him about a legendary old priest who'd scared me to death but from whom I knew I was learning a great deal.

"Yes, Ray's very good," Ted told me. "Very demanding."

He rose from his chair to hand me a yellow major declaration card.

"Your record looks most impressive," he said. "We're happy to have another writer aboard." He walked me to the department office to hand in the card and spent several minutes discussing with me the courses I might take in the future.

Born in Ithaca, New York, Ted had spent his boyhood in the Philippines while his widowed father worked for an American company there. He returned to Ithaca to attend Cornell (I always attributed what I considered to be his refined tastes to these Ivy years), married a coed, and then earned a doctorate from the University of New Mexico before arriving at Loyola to begin teaching. Responsible for most departmental Renaissance courses and his share of sections of freshman composition, it was the Epic course he taught in Loyola's honors program that was his heart's darling. The demands of that honors course were legendary—a full reading of *The Iliad, The Odyssey,* and *La Chanson de Roland,* a graduate-length seminar paper, and more.

I got the feeling that "director of advising" was not a post much sought after, a kind of Siberian assignment, but it suited Ted. He'd taken his sweet time, the full seven years, finishing his degree in Albuquerque, and by his own admission he had not published much since that time. Though he was granted tenure, he had not been promoted beyond the rank of assistant professor in twenty years of service to Loyola. He did not seem bitter, though, more like resigned to the injustice. The English department was by all accounts a hostile place in those days—the dean arbitrated department meetings at one point during my matriculation —and I came to consider myself lucky to have found my way under the wing of someone not interested in university politics but in the care and development of students, who though not a man of any particular faith I knew about had nonetheless embraced the Jesuit mission of *cura personalis,* care of the individual.

The adviser I'd been assigned during my orientation the summer before had been a dumpy, middle-aged religion professor who advised ten or twelve of us en masse in a large auditorium and could not have seemed less interested in me. But Ted was known to startle former students he encountered on Loyola's quadrangles with his amazing recall of their interests, hometowns, even essay topics. He often left messages on my dormitory answering machine about plays and films and musical performances he thought would interest me. Once, while out on a solo jog, he left a worn copy of an obscure novel in my dormitory mailbox, thinking it might help me with a term paper I'd been complaining about. He'd wrapped it in plastic wrap so as not to sweat on it.

I didn't have the pleasure of the Epic course but did take Ted's Renaissance poetry class that first fall I knew him, at his urging. (He'd received me so warmly that afternoon in his office I couldn't resist.) We were assigned E. M. W. Tillyard's *Elizabethan World Picture* and Ovid's *Metamorphoses* before the term even started, then read Donne, Marvell, Herbert, and Shakespeare, poets whose work remained with me verbatim when I sat for the GRE subject test several years later. Ted was a dynamic teacher, often playfully bawdy, leaping like a stage actor as he performed the poems, laughing at our shyness about cruder subjects and language, coaxing us to read the poems aloud anyway. I was out of my depth but was nonetheless an avid participant in class discussion—"The irrepressible Bob," Ted called me. *Plus ca change.* At the end of the term, though, he invited me to sign up for his "Great Figures: Spenser/Milton" course, which I did.

I see now I was an intense young man, more than your average college teacher might want to take on, but Ted took an interest in me like few teachers before or since. One afternoon during that first semester I was in his class, Ted and I passed each other running in Audubon Park and he switched directions to run with me on the dusty bridle path that circles the park's live oaks. It became a regular, more-than-weekly occurrence, and before long he was driving me to local road races and having me to dinner at his house. Sometimes we ran the streetcar tracks, dodging streetcars from Loyola up to Lee Circle and looping back, and when we had the time we ran the five miles from campus along the levee into Jefferson Parish all the way to the Huey P. Long Bridge. I did most of the talking, I'm afraid, about literature, my other classes, love interests, my future. Ted prompted me for more, challenging some of my ideas. Mostly, though, he listened.

Ted's eccentricities must have reminded me of my own father. He'd owned the same three or four suits since his wedding three decades before (something I learned when I accompanied him on a trip to the Oak Street tailor where he had them repaired for twenty years) and carried a very worn leather book satchel that looked to be as old. He spurned driving except when it was absolutely necessary, biking to school instead, and he did not own a television. In his spare time he coached fencing, of all things, and headed up a local badminton club. In a feature I wrote about Ted for a news writing class my junior year, I developed an elaborate conceit that he was another Miniver Cheevy, trapped in his beloved Renaissance, Robinson's days of iron clothing. The news writing teacher, who knew Ted from the racquet club, was amused.

But there was something genuinely compelling for me about a man like Ted Cotton, who seemed to live by the chivalric codes he taught us about. One summer, he asked me to house-sit while he and his wife, Nancy, attended an Alabama Shakespeare festival. They lived on Camp Street, across Audubon Park from the campus, in one of the city's many one-story, turn-of-the-century "shotgun double" homes, built without halls—each room placed behind the other in single file—so that lower- and middle-class homeowners could take advantage of the city's narrow building lots. The long walls of the Camp Street house were lined with bookshelves front to back, except in the kitchen. Music played softly under everything. "It's a library," my girlfriend said while visiting me there. Living there those few days, inhabiting his life, I saw it was the life I wanted. Though I'm sure I sentimentalized things, Ted's existence seemed so simple to me. Full, yes, of all his varied interests, but only those, uncluttered by noise and nonsense. I felt so calm there. Here was my father's farther room, such a mystery all my life. Jane Tompkins says this is that part of what we learn from good teachers, over and above what they talk to us about in class: how to live.

Just before my graduation, while we were running on the levee, Ted let it slip that the Loyola English department had to voted to name me its outstanding senior major at an upcoming honors day. "But I didn't vote for you," he told me. Another student, he said, a classmate from the Renaissance poetry survey several years before, wrote with more complexity than I did, had a better grasp of literary theory, and he had voted for her. I won't say this didn't sting, though winning anyway, without Ted's vote, certainly made it easier to take. And the significance of such things, both the prizes and the disappointments, diminishes greatly as we get older, something I often find myself telling my students these days. Besides, it was an example of Ted's great integrity, something I had grown to depend on from him and that made the great trust between us possible.

An entrance into the world of ideas was probably inevitable for a boy with my background, the son of college teachers, but I have always insisted that the fact that it happened in New Orleans is no accident—my Loyola diploma certifies nothing to me anymore if not that I am an erstwhile New Orleanian. I was so charmed by the place and the pace of life there, where a party guest would as likely ask you where you'd eaten dinner as where you worked or had gone to school. And I believe it's even more crucial that it was Ted who introduced me to this new world. I'm sure my mother felt she was entrusting me to the Jesuits when she packed me off to college, but I now imagine that when my father had abandoned me at Loyola four years before he must have also hoped I would find my way to a teacher like Ted Cotton.

The two men met the day I graduated from Loyola in May 1992. We were all jammed in a small dining room in the student center, a brass band blaring. My father leaned in to speak into Ted's ear. "I admire you," he said, raising his voice above the loud music. It was an enormous gesture for a man like my father, something he probably imagined saying to Ted for a long time, even practiced saying, but something that would have required of him a great emotional effort. Yet it just wasn't in Ted's nature to accept such a compliment. He dismissed it straightaway, said something self-deprecating. Things became awkward, but there was no place for either man to hide. My father slumped in the back seat of our car as I drove my family back to our hotel, the picture of nervous exhaustion.

I stayed in close touch with Ted and all my New Orleans friends after I left town for graduate school. At one point I had a credit card maxed out with nothing but airline tickets back to New Orleans. Ted's frankness with me meant that when I mailed him the earliest drafts of familiar essays I was writing I could take to heart the praise he offered me, praise he'd never offered for the work I'd done in his classes. "I think you've found your métier," he wrote on one draft, and I ran with it.

When my first wife, Anne, and I decided to divorce just as I was beginning the final year of my doctoral program in Nebraska, Ted was the last person I called. Admitting failure to the people I loved and respected was one of the hardest parts of the split for me, and I had a new understanding of why weddings are "witnessed" by family and friends. When I did call Ted, he guessed my bad news (I had not called in so long he'd begun to wonder) and surprised me with some of his own: he and Nancy were divorcing too, after more than thirty-five years. They were to split the Camp Street home, though Nancy would stay on in the house.

Ted asked me about the efficiency apartment on St. Charles Avenue that I had lived in as a college senior, which my best friend, Chris, had taken over after I left town and lived in through his years at the Loyola Law School. Chris was still living at 7825 St. Charles Avenue, Apartment E, but Ted did manage to rent Apartment F, slightly larger and just down the hall. He lived there with his books while he saved to buy another home, and the couple of times I visited the city that year I was able to stay with both men, shuttling back and forth between the two apartments. I loved the feeling I had when I returned to town that very little had changed, that old friends were saving a place for me.

Ted invited me to share Apartment F with him the following summer free of charge, to live on a futon in his living room for the time between my leaving Lincoln and my assuming duties in the English department at St. Lawrence University in northern New York, where I'd taken my first job. It was a good idea. I needed to leave Nebraska but probably wasn't ready for New York and the pressure of a first job just yet. The breakup of my marriage had taken more out of me than I'd expected. Divorce had seemed an expedient solution—Anne and I had no children or assets to divide—but the marriage had revealed to me things about myself, about my capacity for selfishness and cruelty, which I could not put aside right away. Ted and I agreed I could recharge my battery in New Orleans, see old friends, get some writing done.

Even that measly plan proved too ambitious. Ted cooked breakfast for us most mornings that summer, though I was rarely awake to share it with him. My college friends and I caroused most nights, and while they worked by day I was usually to be found in bed or at the Riverbend Daquiri stand near Ted's apartment playing Golden Tee video golf and making long-distance calls from a pay phone there, tying up loose ends back in Lincoln or setting things up in New York, or haggling with May-flower to get my stuff from one place to the other. But once a week or so I did make the effort to get out of bed early and go for a run with Ted along the levee.

"I never thought I'd be here," I said to him over bacon and eggs one of those early mornings. By *here* I guess I meant limbo, or whatever lonesome, purgatorial, not necessarily good place it was I then found myself.

Ted waited a second. "Me either," he finally said once I'd raised my head from my breakfast.

Years before, in the margins of an essay I had mailed to Ted for comment, he had scrawled "You are one of the best male friends of my life-time." I'm afraid I didn't notice the comment until several years later when I went back to revise the piece. So accustomed to Ted anticipating and meeting my needs, so accustomed to his self-sufficiency, even asceticism, it was hard for me to see that summer as his housemate as my chance to repay years of good turns.

My college friends used to tease me about my fifty-year-old friend. Since Ted, I've had a few others—my semipro football coach and my father-in-law, several of my teaching colleagues. I'm not certain about the appeal of these older men, but it's likely that I don't perceive them as threats or rivals they way I do most men my own age. Perhaps also, particularly in Ted's case, I covet their experience and integrity. I had certainly never given any thought to what my appeal to a man like Ted might be.

I guess I was prepared for the two of us to continue playing the roles we'd always played in our friendship: he the gentle master, I the pupil. I know I'm reluctant to move toward the master role with my own students and seem to move in what little authority I have like a boy in a grown man's coat. I still imagine myself the eager, overachieving kid who came to New Orleans with so much to learn and mourn a future that was all potential, no contracted possibilities. Despite all my current happiness, perhaps I envy my students their futures. And Ted's example has been so intimidating. Of my failures at work, I often hear myself say,

"This would never happen to Ted." I suppose my success as a teacher will depend on how well I make this transition, if I ever manage it. It's like I keep waiting for a visit from the integrity fairy that never comes.

Things at Loyola have been good for Ted since my days there. Following something of a regime change in the English department, he was finally promoted to associate professor and awarded the university's highest teaching award, the Dux Academicus. He just concluded a long tenure as director of his beloved honors program, during which one of his brightest students was named a Rhodes Scholar. He eventually bought another beautiful uptown home on Joseph Street where my family and I are frequent guests. (Ted and I still run in the park once in a while when I'm town, though he's had both hips replaced in the last few years and can't run as much as he'd like.)

And he's fallen in love with a wonderful lady, divorced like himself. When he asked me to stand up for them at their wedding, I told him it would be an honor but that I'd have to use in my toast all the things I'd been saving for his eulogy. So much of this is exactly backwards, I am planning to say—me offering advice to him, a sixty-five-year-old man, as he embarks upon a second marriage. The idea of *me* as *his* "best man."

# Capital City

The day after I moved to Lincoln, Nebraska, I took a two-and-a-half-mile run from my downtown apartment out South 13th Street to State Highway 2. In the ten years between the time I left home for college and began my first real job, I lived in four different American cities, communities of all sizes all over the country, and it was a custom of mine to map running routes right away as a means of getting to know the place. It gave me a sense of mastery over the new geography. I logged shorter routes, timed to the minute, for the days when I would be hurried, and I had longer circuits for the days when my calendar was open and I needed to clear my head.

Lincoln is laid out on a simple grid reminiscent of its westward expansion heritage: streets running east and west are lettered A to Z, and streets running north and south are assigned numbers. My first address was the corner of 12th and O Streets, the heart of the city (Allen Ginsberg called O Street "Zero Street" in a derisive poem). That first August evening, I ran east one block and turned down South 13th, which took me past the state's phallic capital building and through a modest, middle-class Lincoln neighborhood. "The Good Life" was the slogan pressed into the Nebraska license plates I saw on cars that lined the streets and filled driveways. I coveted the lawns, the lighted living rooms at dusk. To me, as a middle-class, white male twenty-something, Lincoln seemed to extend the offer of this good life too, in due time.

Two miles out of the heart of Lincoln, I reached its edge. Just past a dying strip mall, Thirteenth Street became a steep grade and widened into four lanes for a brief stretch before it intersected Highway 2. From the top of the hill, I saw how the highway belted the town. I was surprised a city of that size, nearly a quarter-million in population at that time, had an edge so clearly marked. Beyond the highway, on the miles and miles of prairie that seemed to begin where Lincoln ended and run west all the way to Colorado, what Willa Cather called Nebraska's "tableland," there was little to see. Only the state penitentiary marked the landscape. Cather mentions the prison, surely an earlier incarnation, in *O Pioneers!* Alexandra Bergson visits her brother's pitiable murderer, Frank Shabata, there on a mission of forgiveness. The contemporary prison compound, distinguishable from high schools and dormitories only by the fences and razor wire, hardly bears detailed physical description here. What bears noting is how the state pen seemed to loom there at the edge of the Nebraska good life. It looms still in my memories of that place.

Only a month after my arrival in Lincoln, on September 2, 1994, the state of Nebraska planned to execute Harold Lamont "Wili" Otey out at the prison for the June 1977 murder of an Omaha woman named Jane McManus. Walking home from a night of drinking in Omaha, Otey had seen twenty-six-year-old McManus through a window, asleep on her living room sofa. According to the condemned man's own confession, he entered the home through the back door, intending only to steal the woman's stereo. Waking her in the process, though, he proceeded to rape her as well. Otey reported that the victim ultimately pleaded with him to kill her and that he obliged, striking her several times in the head with a hammer and strangling her with a belt. Wili Otey was twenty-five years old and illiterate at the time of the confession. He later recanted, but the state was unmoved.

Otey's would be the first execution in Nebraska since 1959, when one Charlie Starkweather, nineteen-year-old murderer of eleven and inspiration for the Martin Sheen / Sissy Spacek film *Badlands,* had been put to death. During my first month in Lincoln, the Otey case dominated local headlines and news broadcasts and was the talk of the English department at the University of Nebraska, where I was a new graduate assistant. Two women on the department faculty were involved in an organization called Nebraskans Against the Death Penalty, a grassroots group formed in 1990 that opposed Otey's execution and the several slated to follow it. One of those women taught the orientation for new teaching assistants, in which I was required to enroll. She never mentioned the execution in class, but I heard her discussing it with students and colleagues in the hallways before and after class every day.

That's all the case was to me in those days, a conversation in another room only half-perceived. I was at the height of a period of single-minded self-regard then, something America seems to sanction in young people just making their way. That autumn, I was beginning doctoral studies and college teaching and was engaged to be married at the end of that first semester. Both the ideas and the personalities I was encountering at that time excited me, and I could not imagine, I guess, that Wili Otey's life and death had anything to do with mine.

Otey was to be executed at 12:01 A.M. on September 2, a Friday. The state hoped scheduling the event at such an odd hour would discourage crowds. After preparing the next day's classes that Thursday night, I settled in to watch television. My fiancée was still living in Milwaukee and was not to join me in Lincoln until after the December wedding, so I was alone in that half-furnished eighth-floor apartment most of the time. It was not uncommon for me to stay up very late watching old movies or sitcom reruns, as I planned to do that night. I often waited to hear the melancholy theme from *Taxi* at 2:00 A.M. before wandering back to the bedroom.

Local affiliates began to interrupt regular programming just after 10:00 P.M., to initiate the "countdown." The special coverage included interviews with the victim's family, Otey's family, nuns from Kansas who had befriended Wili, attorneys for both sides, law enforcement officers involved with the case; file footage from the twenty-year-old Otey trial, and from the Starkweather case and execution thirty-five years before; tours of the penitentiary, death row, and the chamber housing the electric chair. All of this and periodic live remote broadcasts from the prison parking lot.

The late hour had not, in fact, discouraged crowds—there were throngs pro and con, hundreds strong. It is a great irony, Foucault points out in *Discipline and Punish,* that the public should be so drawn "to a spectacle intended to terrorize it." The group protesting the execution had an air of solemnity at first—praying, singing hymns, bearing candles. Theirs was a vigil. Leaders exhorted them to ignore the pro-execution faction beginning to assemble just across police barricades. "Folks, do you want *them* to be the focus of attention?" one leader yelled. "Just ignore these barbarians."

Ultimately, though, they began to respond to the jeers of the other mob—mostly young men, mostly drunk—whose assembly resembled the bonfire pep rally before a homecoming game. Public execution has carried with it, Foucault reminds, from the time when the accused was put to death before the eyes of the jeering multitudes, "a whole aspect of the carnivalesque, in which rules were inverted, authorities mocked," and the semiprivacy of modern-era American executions seems to make little difference. After trading insults a while, the crowds began to push against each other.

I could not avert my eyes, watched every moment of the broadcast. I had lived in large cities to that point in my life, dangerous ones, even —New Orleans had averaged more than a murder a day during my four years of college there. But I had never before lived in a state capital, in such close proximity to state-sponsored executions. I guess it was the proximity that chilled me. I was a Nebraskan now, albeit a newly minted one, my teaching assistant stipend the equivalent of the state dole when you got down to it, and the sentence to be carried out only miles from where I sat that night, out at the edge of the good and easy life I imagined for myself, would be carried out in my name. The State of Nebraska versus Wili Otey. That weighed heavily on me.

On his way to the chair, Wili Otey stopped at a window in one of the prison's long hallways to wave to his loved ones. Guards gave him a boost so he could see out. Prison officials could not deny that Otey was a changed man since his incarceration and had allowed him to roam the halls of the prison unescorted the last several years. Otey lingered there at the window a moment, I remember.

The execution sequence began at 12:23 A.M., and Otey was pronounced dead ten minutes later. All local stations went to their on-scene reporters for the official pronouncement, and a roar rose from the pro–death penalty carnival. State-appointed media witnesses met for a news conference shortly thereafter. "My opinion has changed on this matter," I remember one middle-aged Omaha reporter saying. The camera panned the cheering crowd outside, and I thought I saw Randy Borg from my 9:30 class bodysurfing atop the arms of the other revelers in his trademark Orlando Magic ball cap.

Randy Borg was like most of the young men I taught in my four years in Lincoln (we were warned in orientation that our classes would be remarkably homogenous in appearance and attitude). Raised in one of Nebraska's small cities like Fremont or Grand Island or Kearney, blue-eyed, blonde-headed Randy Borg had come to the university as a matter of course, the next thing to do, certain that the good life was his birthright and the rest was gravy. A first-generation college student, if I remember right, he was pleasant and polite in class but not much persuaded that my first-year composition class had anything to offer him. Maybe he was right. Thin and tall, Randy sat in the back of the basement classroom in Andrews Hall where our class met every Monday, Wednesday, and Friday morning, slouched so his bony knees were level with his shoulders, the Orlando Magic cap pulled low over his eyes.

I did not sleep well that night under the weight. Mostly, I hoped it had not been Randy I'd seen on the television. Why was that the image from the spectacle that most troubled me? Perhaps identifying Randy brought the case home once and for all, into my living room, finally connected my life to Otey's. I was awakening to the fact that Nebraska's electric chair, as Ted Kooser wrote in a poem later, now sat "in each Nebraskan's home . . . part of our dark oppressive furniture."

Any hope I had of being mistaken about Randy was gone as soon as I saw him the next morning in class, wearing the ball cap and the clothes he'd had on the night before, looking like he had come to class straight from the prison. He sat in the middle of the room surrounded by male classmates, offering them his eyewitness account. "I heard his skin bubbled where they strapped him in," one said. Randy could not confirm it.

I did not know how to proceed; it was not the first time that semester. Our mentors in Nebraska's composition program encouraged us to have students write from their own lives and discouraged broaching the typically polarizing social issues—abortion, gun control, euthanasia, capital punishment—that I had been asked to write about in the freshman writing course I'd taken, "The Analysis of Argument." I did not want to step out of bounds.

"I saw you on TV last night," I finally said to him.

"Yeah?" he said.

"Whether or not you think the guy deserved it," I said, "didn't it strike you as a solemn occasion?"

"That's just the media making you feel that way," Randy said.

On September 1, 1979, my former first-grade classmate and friend Cary Ann Medlin was kidnapped, molested, and murdered, stabbed in the neck with a pocketknife. She was eight. The night Wili Otey died in Lincoln, almost fifteen years to the day after Cary's murder, thirty-eight-year-old Robert Glen Coe awaited lethal injection on Tennessee's death row for killing her.

Cary Medlin had moved the year before her death from my small West Tennessee hometown of Martin to an even smaller one ten miles away, a farm and factory community of 2,200 called Greenfield. Cary was riding bikes with her stepbrother in a Greenfield church parking lot that September afternoon when a friendly young man pulled up in a Gran Torino, just like the one my mother drove in those days. In a confession dated a few days after the murder (which Coe, like Otey, later disavowed), Coe, then twenty three, explained that he'd left his job at a local garage early, itching to find someone to flash. He had been picked up for that before. Finding no one, he pulled up to Cary Ann Medlin, convinced her he knew her stepfather and needed her help finding him, and coaxed her into the car to help him search. He drove her a few miles to Bean Switch Road, a shady lover's lane that runs along a soybean field. "Jesus loves you," Cary told Coe as he killed her. After a day's search, a crew of investigators and local men found her body in a weedy corner of that field, the sort of field the railroad engineer must have had in mind when, passing through on the Illinois Central tracks decades before, he gave the town its name.

I cannot adequately eulogize Cary Medlin here. I was myself only nine when she was killed. What her parents have said of her in the local papers is true. Like most young girls, she was sweet, bubbly, quick to trust. I remember one summer day the year before her death, my parents brought us to the swimming pool at the apartment complex where Cary was living with her family because the city pool down the street from our house was being renovated. When she spotted me, she stopped pedaling and straddled her bike, calling to me from the chain-link fence. "Hey, Bobby Cowser!" she yelled cheerily. "What are you doing here?" We had both just finished second grade.

My mother stood in our driveway discussing the murder with a neighbor the day we heard. I was as sad as a nine-year-old boy could be, I suppose. I ran to find my yearbook and looked a long time at Cary's photo in order to remember her better. I thought of the day at the University Courts pool. Ever the good boy, I recall making note of the mistakes Cary had made by allowing Coe to separate her from her stepbrother and by getting into a stranger's car. One was taught, at home and school, to be more careful.

I was aware from a young age that I lived in a violent place. Cary's death was the first but not the only time murder touched my young life. Years later, Marlena Childress, the niece of a classmate, also disappeared, though her body was never found. Marlena's mother's story changed several times—first it was that Marlena had been kidnapped, then the mother said she had sold her for drug money, then said that wasn't true. On a tip, authorities dragged the North Fork of the Obion River for days but turned up nothing. The case made it on Robert Stack's *Unsolved Mysteries.* Harold Powell, a Mohawked bully from my neighborhood, was convicted of the murder of a local college student during my freshman year of high school. He said it was self-defense, that the man had made a pass at him so he clubbed him with a dumbbell, but that did not explain how Harold ended up driving the dead man's Firebird. He got thirty-eight years for second-degree murder and a handful of lesser charges. When our civics teacher, Mr. Bragg, took on us on a field trip to the Lake County Regional Correctional Center some time after, I recognized Harold's curly red Mohawk under the backboard in the prison gymnasium, where he awaited a rebound. "Bobby Cowser," Harold called to me, clutching the basketball, "what are *you* doing here?!"

Like the Otey execution, the execution of Robert Glen Coe would be the first in Tennessee in decades, since 1960. Though the condemned in America usually exhaust all avenues of appeal in ten to twelve years and though 70 percent of Tennesseans surveyed were in favor of the death penalty, Coe ultimately survived more than twenty years on death row at the Riverbend Maximum Security Institute outside Nashville. Cary Medlin's mother, Charlotte Stout, a nurse auditor, began to lose patience. She lay the blame at the feet of federal judge John Nixon, a Carter appointee. As she could not campaign to have him voted out of office, Mrs. Stout, darling of victims' rights groups, led a call for Nixon's impeachment. She went all the way to Washington to testify before a judicial subcommittee that though states like Texas had successfully executed dozens of inmates since the Supreme Court reinstated capital punishment, Judge Nixon had, because of matters of personal conscience, consistently thwarted justice when capital cases came before him. He'd even accepted awards for his advocacy.

A graduate of Harvard and Vanderbilt Law School, Nixon is a liberal Democrat, a veteran of LBJ's Justice Department and the civil rights movement and son of one of the original contributors to the Agrarian manifesto *I'll Take My Stand,* and he likens judicial execution to nuclear weapons: something you would like to have in your arsenal but should employ reluctantly. Nixon went so far as to overturn Coe's conviction at one point, on the grounds that the jury in his original case had been improperly directed, but a higher court overruled him. In response to complaints, capital cases were eventually routed around Nixon's bench. The judge went on senior status in 1999, a kind of partial retirement.

Editorials in the *Weakley County Press* called for a swift end to Charlotte Stout's suffering, while news articles never feigned journalistic objectivity. Greenfield's overalled old guard spoke in the *Memphis Commercial Appeal* in informal interviews from Wimpy's Corner on Main Street. They were sick of appeals. "Fry the bastard," one man said, apparently unaware that the state had elected to use lethal injection. "No, turn him loose on Main Street and give us fifteen minutes notice," said another, a game warden who helped in the search for Cary's body. "If he'd done that to my kid, he'd have never made it to trial."

Coe was finally executed on April 19, 2000. The demonstration outside the Riverbend Institute was nothing like what I had seen in Lincoln, according to reports. Two hundred people assembled, mostly anti–death penalty protesters. Charlotte Stout convinced prison officials to convert a special room in Riverbend so she could see the execution of her daughter's killer live, rather than on a video monitor as was the standard procedure. Reading about the event the next morning on the Internet, recognition startled me again: listed among the media witnesses to the execution was Paul Tinkle, manager of the Martin radio station WCMT and play-by-play announcer for my high school football games; the Reverend Schuyler J. McCracken, erstwhile teenage umpire of the Little League that played its games across the street from my house, waited outside the prison to minister to Coe's grieving family.

The year after Otey's execution, I was working in Lincoln with a summer program for Nebraska high school writing teachers. First thing each morning, we arranged ourselves in a circle and read from what we had written the night before. One particular morning, Kip, a middle-aged Omaha middle school teacher, shared a sentimental poem about his basset hound, who had wandered into the path of an oncoming car. "The dog was a member of our family," Kip explained. The teacher next to him wept openly. It was her turn next. She wiped her eyes. Her piece was a letter to the editor. John Joubert, convicted murderer of two Omaha paperboys, was scheduled to be executed in a matter of weeks, the first since Wili Otey. "Fry the bastard" was her gist; "What's the holdup?"

I moved away from Lincoln, Nebraska, several years ago now, to live the good life in a cozy house on a small river in northern New York. It is hard to imagine my life has anything whatsoever to do with Wili Otey's, or Robert Coe's, but walking past my house at evening you may see the Nebraska electric chair figured prominently there in my lighted living room, lugged all the way from Lincoln in my imagination.

Sitting in that living room, I can hardly think of Lincoln without imagining the state pen looming at the edge of memory, without seeing Wili Otey's irreducible, always human face peering from the small window that last time, without seeing the smug but human face of blue-eyed Randy Borg, even. I imagine Mohawked bully Harold Powell asking, more plaintive now, "Bobby Cowser, what are you doing here?" The Reverend Schuyler McCracken, good old Sky McCracken from my childhood, telling a reporter, "Robert Coe wasn't comfortable with his soul in this world, but I know he's right with it now." And little Cary Ann Medlin from Mrs. Thomason's first-grade class, out in that green field of soybeans, saying, "Jesus loves you." The unlikeliest voice of mercy in all this.

# (Never) Going Back
# to My Old School

I began to think about my ten-year high school reunion around the time my older sister, Mary, had to decide whether she would be attending hers. She was working in New York City at the time, a university admissions counselor living in an apartment on Fish Avenue in the Bronx, and I was visiting her from Milwaukee on spring break. We were riding a university shuttle bus in to her Manhattan office when the subject came up. Organizers of her reunion had contacted my parents about her whereabouts.

Mary said simply she wasn't going. Not interested. I knew from looking at the photo albums in her apartment that week, the photographs of ex-boyfriends conveniently if conspicuously removed, that Mary would be able to resist the curiosity Japanese ethnographer Keiko Ikeda says draws Americans back to their high school reunions. She would have had little trouble, based on what I saw, entering a witness relocation program. But I wondered there on the Pelham Parkway, even two years out from my own reunion, even if going back was a terrible idea (and it was), whether I could resist attending my own.

Martin seemed to take stronger hold of each my parents' children as you descended the birth order, so that Jimmy might be considered the truest "Martian," having stayed home for college and retained a thick Tennessee accent. But Mary seemed pointed toward an East Coast education almost from the moment she started high school. She was a textbook overachiever—top ten in her graduating class, a Girl Scout Gold Award recipient, volunteer at the local food bank and in local political campaigns, a dependable babysitter. I don't doubt she was genuinely committed to these projects, but I knew each had a place on her college applications too. Westview High seemed something she'd endured and put behind her right away when she left town for Boston College.

Me, I'm afraid I had more trouble moving on after my time at Westview was up. Not that my days there were filled with glory. I graduated twenty-ninth out of some 150 kids in the class of '88 (twenty-ninth-atorian, I dubbed myself). I think it's more that my high school days were such a disappointment that's made them hard for me to let go of. Try as I might, I'd just never really felt a part of things there.

I harbor a healthy suspicion of all of these sentimental experiences we're told should frame our lives—proms, beauty pageants, class reunions. I mean, the 101st Airborne has something to get excited about at their reunions, but the class of '88? Nor did I relish the idea of placing myself once again under the critical gaze of peers so influential in the development of what was the not-so-good self-image I carried forward from adolescence. Though I'd been home often in the ten years since leaving Martin, I'd hardly ventured out of my parents' house except to exercise or gather supplies. My sisters and I actually hid from former classmates we saw at the Martin Wal-Mart. Still, it's hard for me to dismiss these frames altogether. Kurt Vonnegut claims high school is the core of the American experience, for better or worse. Even now, I find myself commenting how much this or that academic committee reminds me of being on the yearbook staff.

I had managed to finish my Ph.D. and start my first college teaching job only weeks before my own reunion. That's mostly coincidence, though Ikeda says the other chief reason people attend high school reunions, beyond curiosity, is to "show off" their own achievements. Maybe I'd pushed to finish in time to crow about the degree and the job at the reunion. My divorce had been finalized that year also, and I probably didn't want to show up empty-handed either, with only my failures to talk about.

I arrived in Nashville on a Friday afternoon, the reunion's festivities set to begin with a family picnic during the day Saturday and the banquet itself to take place later Saturday night. The Westview Charger football team had a road date that night in McKenzie, Tennessee, so after dinner out with my parents I excused myself to catch part of the ball game. The Chargers were largely also-rans during my time on the team, but since then they had become a regional power, a perennial state playoff team, and had two players on NFL rosters. They were certainly having their way with the poor McKenzie Rebels that warm autumn evening.

Standing down under a goalpost, I saw my old teammate Sandy Coleman by himself in the stands, and he motioned me up to where he was sitting. He was working out at the Hubbell Lighting plant on the Old Fulton Highway, he told me, where he'd been practically since our graduation. He'd apprenticed for a while with a tool and die maker in Pennsylvania right after high school. "But I just missed Martin too much," he said, and so moved back home to marry his high school sweetheart and work at Hubbell alongside his father. He and his wife, Missy, had two young children, and the couple would own their home outright in about five years.

Sandy guessed I was in town for the reunion but told me that he wasn't going. "Bobby, I see these people all the time," he told me. I couldn't have said who his best friend had been back in our school days. Had he even gone to the prom? Missy, several years behind us in school, likely wouldn't know anybody at the reunion. "My kids got their own activities," he said.

We talked a little about our football fortunes back in the day. I offered that we'd been talented but poorly coached. Sandy agreed, but I could see, when I really bared my teeth on the subject, that I crossed some line with him, and that he felt a little sorry for me, who had no house mortgage and no family. "Long time ago now," he said, looking pretty uncomfortable, turning back to the game.

I thought a lot about Sandy's reaction on the drive home. I recently came across an advice column in an old issue of *Redbook* magazine offering an eleven-point program for dealing with high school reunions. "Don't obsessively announce how you've changed and or were misunderstood" is point #3. The next morning I still wasn't sure I was in the right frame of mind for the reunion. Maybe I'd stay home after all.

I decided I could test the water at the family picnic held at the elementary school playground just down the street from my parents' house. If that went badly, I told myself, I'd just spend the night with my parents. They said it made no difference to them whether I went to the reunion or not, but I suspected my mother would have been happy to have me stay home, fearing contact with that high school element might compromise what she certainly considered my "recovery."

So just after lunch, I walked down to the playground and wandered to where the nattily dressed children of other classmates were eating dirt under the swing set. While my ten years in college and graduate school seemed to prolong my adolescence, I could see my classmates had pushed full steam ahead into middle-class life. I honestly couldn't have imagined landing a house mortgage at that point in my life, not to mention raising children. Only a few payments into my first car loan, I was thinking in terms of baby steps.

Our class president and organizer of the reunion was my best high school friend, Andy Blackwell, and he was the first adult I spoke to that afternoon at the playground. Andy was a handsome second-generation Baptist preacher, a real straight-arrow superhero type, mustached since the seventh grade. "Bear," we called him, for his hairiness and the way he growled through calisthenics on the football field. That's where I'd gotten to know him, on the gridiron, and we were immediate running buddies, me riding shotgun in his shiny gold Pontiac Fiero all over Weakley County. He stayed at home for college, and after dating, best anybody could figure, every available girl in a three-county area (including my sister Ruth just after we'd graduated), he married another girl from Ruth's class and was holding their three-year-old daughter, Savannah, in his arms as we spoke. They were also parents to a little boy, Jameson. Along with his ministry, Andy told me he was substitute teaching at another high school in the county, held onto a few city mowing contracts from his college days, and now owned a hundred or so head of cattle for extra money.

I told him a little about my new teaching job. Andy had been a groomsman in my wedding in St. Louis three years before, so we also spoke a little about the divorce. I told him Anne was doing well so far as I knew, living in Chicago and earning more than I was. A pretty amicable parting, as divorces go. What could I tell him? That our life together became ordinary almost right away, and that I was beginning to understand I'd left to avoid the image of myself I saw in my wife's face, stripped of rationalizations and grand delusions. I suspect my trepidation about the reunion had something to do with my fear of seeing this stripped-down version myself in the faces of my classmates.

Andy told me about a tour of the brand-new high school building that his committee had planned, but I said I thought I'd skip that, go home and watch some football.

"You've got a beautiful family, Andy," I told him before leaving. "I'm glad it's all going so well for you. You're a lucky man."

"It's not luck, Bobby," he said quickly. "It's Jesus."

I had hoped to see my high school girlfriend, Rachel Forgy, at the picnic. Perhaps it's better to say that of all the people I thought I might see at the reunion, she was one about whom I was acutely curious. I had heard she was at the playground with her Nashville optometrist husband and their children but hadn't managed to run into her. Rachel and I dated on and off through our senior year until she ended things once and for all while we were on separate senior trips in Florida, so she could begin seeing a guy she'd met on the beach at Panama City. It strikes me now as something out of a John Hughes film, something laughable, but at the time it was terrible, ruined my trip and that whole summer until I left home for New Orleans. I didn't take it well at all.

She chose a Christian school in Nashville for college. I saw her during Thanksgiving break the next year at an impromptu reunion some of my classmates were having at a UT-Martin fraternity house where they'd pledged that term, on the arm of the guy she'd dated immediately before taking up with me, a guy I have to admit I always considered a rival. Sometime after that, during a real lull in my romantic life, I wrote Rachel a letter asking what she thought had gone wrong between us. "Too young to feel the feelings we felt," she wrote back, something sensible I was sure she'd heard from her parents. When her wedding announcement appeared in the *Press* a few years later while I was home on a vacation, my mother tried to hide the paper from me.

I sat in my parents' living room the rest of that afternoon waiting for the rush of courage that would send me out the door to the reunion. When my mother left to buy wine and cigarettes tax-free across the border in Fulton, Kentucky, I asked her to pick up a small bottle of pricey vodka for me just in case. "I don't go back to Martin often," a former classmate wrote to me in an E-mail just the other day, a girl I remembered as having been very popular, a cheerleader. "It's so boring and intimidating." Yes, intimidating, exactly, but why? Such a tiny, unimportant place, a veritable speck on the map. And boring to boot.

The girl I was dating at the time of the reunion was a flight attendant who'd arranged for me to fly free, but I strongly discouraged her from coming along (a good call, according to *Redbook*—no dates, no spouses). I told her it was something I needed to do alone. "It's not like it's a gunfight," she told me. Fair enough. But I knew no matter how far and wide I had traveled, no one I ever met seemed as real to me as the people I'd known as a child back in Martin, people who are the archetypes, according to Vonnegut, for everybody else we'll ever meet. Intimidating stuff. I just couldn't decide what would be worse, the way I'd feel at seeing Rachel again, for instance—that cold-wind-blowing-through-me feeling—or never feeling it at all, never satisfying my curiosity. Fading away.

I ended up going to the reunion. Of course I did. The rush of courage never came, but I guess I decided I couldn't bury my head my whole life, hide from the newspaper, take pictures out of my photo albums and pretend people and things, things like divorces, hadn't happened to me. I drove my mother's tanklike Chevy Caprice Classic ten miles or so west of Martin to a small banquet hall in Union City, Tennessee, wearing a coat but no tie, that bottle of vodka tucked under the passenger seat.

Once inside the hall, I found a long folding table full of name badges, searched for mine (it read "Bobby Cowser—Professor"), and spent some time scanning the other names there. "Cocktail hour," one of the waitstaff informed me as he passed. "Dinner to follow." I expected the we'd be served the things we'd had at banquets in high school—rolls, salad (read: lettuce), catfish or smoked ham (local specialties), iced tea to drink.

Our teachers were no real presence that night, the way they'd been at proms and other dances. I made my way to the group of guys I'd hung around with at Westview, the guys from the senior trip. We exchanged informal résumés, as it were. Warren Hamner, now a chemical engineer, introduced me to his wife as "the guy who beat me out for 'wittiest.'" Drew Kim had heard of St. Lawrence University, where I had just begun teaching, having roomed with a guy at Amherst who wore a St. Lawrence sweatshirt, a gift from a sister who'd gone there. He said he was attending the Duke School of Public Policy now, and I told him I'd heard of that too. I told Benjamin Gilmer I'd seen a name badge at the table announcing he was a physician. He seemed surprised at this news but pleased, and didn't offer to elaborate. Point #2 on the *Redbook* list advises reunion-goers to be evasive if not exactly misleading about achievements. Maybe Benjamin had read it. But I found that I couldn't help but play down my "accomplishments," even if I'd come to flaunt them. "No, no, I don't live in New York City," I heard myself tell several people. "A far cry." And I made sure Drew understood I was teaching at St. Lawrence and not Sarah Lawrence. "We wish we were Sarah Lawrence," I told him, even though that's probably not true.

I did finally get the chance to speak to Rachel. She'd seen me across the room and made her way to me through the small circles of our chatting classmates, a broad smile on her face. If every other aspect of this experience had tended to underwhelm, to be a bit of an anticlimax, seeing Rachel again was exactly as I had imagined.

"How are you?" I began, reaching out to hug her. "You look good."

"I'm great," she said. "Mark and I have two little girls. I'm teaching preschool art classes." She did look good, I have to say, unchanged in all the time since I'd seen her. The cold wind, big time. I could see her husband watching us with some interest from across the room.

"I have no trouble imagining that," I said.

"So you're a professor," she asked, glancing up from my name badge. "Whereabouts?"

I gave her the details. I could see in her face she wanted things to be okay with us. Not intimate, decidedly not that, but okay. Nice. Pleasant.

"You always had talent in that direction," she finally said, and I thanked her.

As dinner began, I found myself seated at the head table with Andy and Melissa Blackwell, class president and first lady. It became clear that the keg of beer I had seen in the corner when I arrived (I'd already helped myself to a couple of glasses) was no small bone of contention for the members of the reunion committee. Teetotaler Andy had objected strenuously during the planning meetings and seemed very unpleasantly surprised the beer had appeared anyway. Melissa was trying to settle him down. I heard one of the ladies at our table saying Disney had been wonderful but that she and her husband were just too big to walk it anymore. "So what are you doing now, Bobby?" Monica Reese asked me, just as I bit into a dinner roll.

I saw the DJ's wireless microphone making its way to a table in the back of the room a few minutes later and heard a classmate in the back fiddling with the on/off switch. "We're going to take some time now to tell one another what we've been up to," he said. One by one, each of the one hundred from our class in attendance offered a little progress report on his or her life—children, spouses, promotions, and other milestones. It was the only thing on the program besides dinner and dancing. "I did not have sex with that woman, Miss Lewinsky," Drew

Kim announced when the microphone came to him. Tommy Gallien explained he'd been married and divorced and got only the dog and the mustard in the settlement. I cringed even as I laughed at that one.

I thought about what I was going to say when it came my turn. I suppose I'd dreamed about a moment like that one for a long time, that the dream probably kept me going many times in the last decade when I would have otherwise let go the rope. If I was going to have any great, cathartic moment that weekend, this would have been it.

But what I'd come to see over the course of that weekend was that my accomplishments, while they meant a great deal to me, were not likely to make a deep impression on those gathered. Anybody who thought about me at all since high school, from what I could tell, had done so only fondly, which ruined my living-well-as-revenge fantasy. I saw I was like the boy in "Araby," driven and derided by vanity.

The last to speak, I took the microphone from Andy, who'd thanked his Lord and savior and asked us to remember those from our class who'd passed on.

"Yes, well," I began, looking out on the expectant faces. "I'm divorced myself. I've moved back in with my parents a short time ago and spend most of the day in my bathrobe, watching soap operas and eating cold cereal. But I'm very glad to be here with you tonight."

A few people laughed, those who knew better. I can only guess the rest believed it. We were a nice group of people, but in the ways that counted we hardly knew one another at all anymore. I handed the microphone back to Andy, who looked a little stunned.

The rest of the evening, well, I have a handle only on the lowlights. All denouement anyway. "Don't overextend yourself alcoholically," advises *Redbook*. Things on the dance floor picked up. I was surprised to see Rachel and her husband out on the floor—her fundamentalist father had forbidden her to dance at our senior prom, so we stayed only an hour and she rode home in tears. I went to Mom's car and got the vodka and proceeded to dance myself out of my coat and shirt and shoes. Kerry Kelly, now a Nashville hairdresser, helped me finish off the bottle. Andy Blackwell left without saying goodnight to anyone.

When the reunion broke up at ten, someone brought me to an after party out in the Glenwood subdivision, only it was a party thrown by folks in town for their fifteen-year reunion. They didn't seem to mind, considered the handful of us from the '88 reunion a novelty, until I broke up the party by falling backwards off the deck trying to swig from a wine bottle. I remember very little of the Backside Pub, where we touched down next, the only place in town where you could legally purchase a mixed drink, though I do remember Brad Smith helping me out of his car and up to my parents' back door. *Redbook* point #11: "Find a group of people to leave with."

As fate would have it, my flight out of Nashville the next morning was an early one and had my father and me leaving Martin before eight. My mother had to jostle me violently to get me out of bed. When I got out of the shower, she was still in my old bedroom, sitting on the bed. I could see she wanted to proceed carefully.

"Honey," she said, "where's my car?"

The kind of question you never imagine you'll have to ask your grown college professor son, I'm sure. I blanked at first, but then remembered the ride from Brad Smith.

"Backside Pub," I told her. I was fairly certain.

My dad and brother set out to retrieve it. I apologized to my mother for losing the car and the haste with which I threw my things together and got out of there.

All the way to Nashville, I fought the urge to ask my dad to pull over on the roadside so I could be sick. Not a very dignified way to go out, I know, though even then, looking out at the pink Tennessee morning, I began to see the weekend had been something of a purge, nasty but necessary, that with all that high school stuff behind me now perhaps I could move forward.

# My Double, My Brother

*A brother . . . gives us more skin—thicker skin sometimes, thinner skin sometimes.*

John Edgar Wideman

During my senior year in high school, just before Christmas, my father received a phone call from a woman in Houston, a woman he'd never heard of, who told him his younger brother, R. L., was dying in a hospital there and if Dad wished to see his brother, she was afraid he'd need to come to Texas right away. She wasn't sure calling my father was the right thing—R. L. had asked her not to. But she couldn't bear to see him go alone.

Only a few years apart in age, my dad and his brother were extraordinarily close while they were growing up in rural East Texas in the thirties and forties. They were, in a way, my grandparents' second generation of children, born twenty years after the first, my aunts Juanita and Fleda. The boys heard their parents say to friends and guests, in fact, that they'd conceived R. L. as a playmate for my father, himself a bit of a surprise. The teenaged sisters had a hand in naming and raising their brothers: they lobbied to name my father Bobby Gene after the younger brother of one of their friends; R. L. had no actual name, only the initials.

I've always thought how the two men seemed to be doubles. My father was the first member of the family to leave their farm for college a few miles away in Commerce, Texas, and R. L. followed him there only a few years after. They both did graduate degrees in English, both eventually became professors after stints in high school classrooms. They looked alike too, though I don't recall my uncle being as bald or as slight as my father.

There was a more fundamental difference: while my father's teaching took him to Connecticut, where he met and married my mother and started our family, R. L. stayed in Texas, taught his whole career at a junior college outside of Houston, and remained a lifelong bachelor. He smoked rich-smelling cigars, covered the ballet for Houston newspapers, and was a world traveler. I remember the photos of himself he sent to us, taken on the decks of tankers bound for exotic places like Turkey.

Once during an extended visit with us, my uncle announced flatly (and apparently apropos of nothing) that he'd never marry. My mother was nonplussed by the remark and feared it was prompted by the harried life he saw around him that week—my three siblings and I were then in the throes of adolescence. If he meant offense by his remark, it would seem that he softened during his last days. "At least you have those kids to leave behind," he said to my father from what turned out to be his deathbed.

R. L. did not live until Christmas. Systemic cancer, my parents told us. I guess my reaction to his death was typical for my age. I wondered why I did not feel worse. Some weeks after the death, my uncle's friends mailed to my father a videotape of the memorial service held in R. L.'s honor. My dad asked if I might like to view it with him. It had been a windy day in Wharton, Texas, and both the audio and video were terrible. I soon lost interest and left my father alone to watch the video on the VCR he'd rented.

The oddest thing is that my father had not been present for my uncle's actual death. After Dad had been in Houston several days, R. L. told him he realized Dad would need to get back—to family and to classes. He should go, R. L. said. But they would not say goodbye. What my uncle wanted, when the time came, was for my father to leave the hospital room without a word, as though he were headed for the men's room, then never come back. My father complied. I imagine my father exiting the hospital the way a boy leaves a matinee—opening the doors to harsh light.

Dad did not go directly home but went next to R. L.'s place and spent a couple of days there gathering my uncle's effects. He found tins full of quarters all over the apartment —$200 worth. The diamond ring and watch my uncle had always worn so proudly, my father learned from a Houston jeweler, were fakes. Dad left instructions that a line from Chaucer's Prologue to *The Canterbury Tales,* a line about the lonesome Clerk, be chiseled on R. L.'s headstone—"gladly would he learn / and gladly teach." You can't make it out on the grainy video.

I get most of the details of that story from my own brother, Jimmy. During the weeks after my Uncle R. L. died, Dad drove Jimmy to junior high on McComb Street in the family Monte Carlo, as he'd done all that school year. Though we'd had the car probably three years by that time, my father hadn't yet learned to operate the cassette player, so in the weeks after my uncle died, Dad began to ask my brother to cue his Whitney Houston tape to play "The Greatest Love of All" while they rode to the school. Dad wept quietly all the way, Jim says (though he never did at home, not a tear), then stopped crying abruptly as he reached the doors of the school and drove on to the office.

I often rely on my brother's insight when it comes to Dad. Jimmy was at home several years after I left for college and was present for things I missed, things like those rides to school. My dad makes sense to my brother in a way he never has to me; Jim understands Dad's

Depression-era austerity (my father is a man of tight budgets—financial and emotional). I sensed my brother felt a bit guilty even telling me this particular story. He was violating a trust, going over budget.

Years after my uncle died, after all three of my siblings and I had left home for college, my father appeared in the doorway of my parents' kitchen one afternoon and spoke to my mother in much the same way my uncle had years before, when he'd announced his intention never to marry. Dad addressed her, she says, as though she had been privy to a lengthy conversation he'd clearly been having only with himself. He seemed to have surfaced from a deep well of grief. "I realize I'm all alone now," he told her.

"All evidence to the contrary aside," my mother says to me wryly over the phone weeks later, as a sort of punch line to the story. "What about me? What about you kids?" she says. But I think I understand what my father meant.

I used to have nightmares as a little boy about losing my brother. When he was four or five years old, spending a day with my mother at the municipal pool down the street from our house, Jimmy leapt from the high dive feet first onto the head of another boy whom he'd not seen swim out from under the board. My mother was there, across the pool, and saw the whole thing, saw my brother bob to the surface, face still submerged. Imagine her panic: she yells and yells at busy lifeguards before diving in herself to get him. She drags a limp Jimmy to the pool deck. A living nightmare. And that was how mine always began: Jimmy face down in the pool. It was the worst thing I could imagine.

Unlike my father and Uncle R. L., who'd re-created dogfights from World War II's European theater with planes they fashioned them-selves from balsa, Jimmy and I were not really playmates as little boys, something that worried my mother. My brother was four years young-er than me, yet he was like the older brother in every other way. He had friends older than I was, he complained of me snooping through his things, and he had generally no time for or interest in a relationship with me.

Something happened, though, between the time I left home for college at eighteen and the year Jimmy and I lived together in Lincoln, Nebraska, when I was twenty-six and finishing graduate school. The inertia of simple heredity, perhaps. Jim's first marriage had ended after just a year, and my own was quietly dissolving. I had only qualifying exams and the dissertation remaining on the degree, and I imagined Jimmy and I could both use the company, so I offered him the classic soft place to fall. He accepted, and my poor mother began to pray nightly to St. Monica, patroness of mothers and mother of St. Augustine, the world's original lecher.

We were not so bad. We spent a lot of time in the cab of his truck that year, side by side. We were fleeing the less than happy facts of our lives, to be sure, but we were also chasing down films, rock and roll shows, and football games—in short, pursuing zealously interests we had not previously known were common. Frankly, I enjoyed the time we spent together in the truck the most. Sometimes we just drove to drive, like we'd done in high school. The truck's cab felt as complete and entire as the perfect unpierced yolk of an egg, and somehow as fragile. Inside we spoke easily and listened well to each other. Or we listened wordlessly to what was playing on the radio. *Simpatico.* It seemed uncanny to both of us how, by the time we came to live together again, we'd come to so greatly resemble one another, physically and otherwise, like twins you read about who are separated at birth and when reunited later find they prefer exactly the same chewing gum. When we arrived at our various destinations, even when we stopped for gas, I hated to open the truck's door, to break the cab's seal.

Our likeness was a great consolation to me that year. To admire oneself is, of course, unseemly, but in as much as a boy's brother is his double, admiring your brother is a way of embracing what you consider good in yourself and your family. I had wanted to say something like that when I toasted my brother and his first bride years before at their wedding, but it was too much talking. Instead I told the assembled guests about my earliest lucid memory: spring evening, rectangular banks of windows high on our living room wall send narrow shafts of light, at angles, to the floor; my mother, pregnant with Jimmy, rests beneath these shafts of light, on a brown couch flush against the wall of our living room; and my sisters and I take turns listening to the April baby stir.

Several years ago while visiting my parents for Christmas, I went to check my E-mail in the small bedroom where my father had assembled his computer. The desk in the makeshift office was piled with manila folders full of writing: typescript poems in various stages of incompletion, handwritten reminiscences my father had begun but abandoned, unfinished letters to my siblings and me (he, by and large, spurns talking to us by phone because of the cost), a few spiral journals he keeps while on the day trips he likes to take around Tennessee and Kentucky now that he's retired. My mother calls Dad "the family scribe."

Among those folders I found one labeled "R. L.'s Texas Teachers Annuity." My uncle had been dead more than ten years by that time. Upon my uncle's death, my father, as sole surviving relative, became beneficiary of R. L.'s generous retirement annuity. Actually, I think it was we, my father's children, who benefited. My uncle had been generous in life—my father heard tell during his time in Houston of the terrific New Year's parties R. L. threw, to which he invited anyone and everyone who'd entertained him over the course of that year and at which he served champagne by the case. R. L. sent each of my siblings and me an embarrassingly large check every Christmas and set money aside so that each of us could spend two weeks touring Europe after our graduation from high school, though he only lived to see my older sister actually make the trip, and though my brother ultimately convinced my dad to let him use the travel money as a down payment on a new Nissan truck instead of going abroad.

But it was after his death when R. L.'s generosity was most deeply felt. During the ten-year period when my parents had at least one and sometimes three children enrolled in college at any given time, R. L.'s annuity saved my parents, at least allowed their children the private educations my parents had dreamed about us having. "I don't know what we'd have done without student loans and R. L.'s retirement," my mother is fond of saying. I like to think this was the kind of legacy my uncle hoped to have.

I did not expect, when I opened the annuity file, to find R. L.'s death certificate on top of the stack of papers inside. In the upper right corner of the form was a box for "cause of death." My eyes stopped there. Kaposi's sarcoma.

Honestly, it was not surprise I felt in that moment. Nor did I feel deceived. Instead I felt a vague sense of confirmation, and an accompanying calm. It was as though I was slowly realizing a truth that had been before me always but that eluded me, like so many family secrets, until I was ready for it. I had spoken to my mother and brother in the time since my uncle's death about precisely the possibilities I was considering just then—one, almost certain, that my uncle had died of complications from AIDS, and another, certainly not automatic, that the lifelong bachelor had been gay. All the circumstantial, stereotypical evidence pointed to those assumptions: it seemed to explain my uncle's bachelorhood, his acute sensitivity to innocent questions we asked him (when we were very small) about girlfriends, his desire to keep my father in the dark about his illness.

I also felt the slow burn the snoop always feels when he's uncovered what he must have been looking for: the death certificate's secret, like all ill-gotten evidence, was inadmissible, not something I could safely bring up at the holiday table. Still, the bittersweetness of snooping success never deters me.

I closed the file folder and walked out into the rest of the house. It was late in the morning. My mother was alone in the kitchen, stooped over the dishwasher. I told her how I'd come across the death certificate, and the sarcoma diagnosis.

"I didn't know they listed that," she said. She seemed to know what was coming.

"So, Mom," I finally said, "Uncle R. L. died of AIDS?"

"Yes," she said, without much hesitation. "But you guessed that years ago." As I say, I had broached the subject with her before, during college.

"I just asked if he'd been gay," I said, "and you said you didn't know."

"It was your father's story to tell," she told me, her head back in the dishwasher.

Or his secret to keep.

I have not kept my brother's secrets, such as they are. In fact, I am afraid it may be said I have "dined out" on them.

The first story I told about my brother was at a high school baseball game at Harmon Field. It was early spring, still cold, the gray sky resting on the field like a lid. The girls from my high school sat on the top rows of the bleachers, many wearing the shiny baseball windbreakers that belonged to the boys in the dugout and on the field.

I sat below them on the bleachers, a few rows down, more jester than courtier, and tried to make myself compelling. I remember sitting below Shonna Sexton that particular day, having turned myself completely away from the field and toward her. Shonna's face was small and heart-shaped, and she always laughed easily with me. She was pretty and bright and worthy of my longing.

Shonna seemed to look both at me and beyond me at first, hardly in rapt attention. Until I began giving up the goods on my family, people she knew a great deal about already because she and my younger sister, Ruth, were good friends and both members of the high school cheerleading squad. I told the story of how my brother had exacted revenge for my shaming him in front of his friends a few nights before. Because of my size and age advantage, the usual routes of revenge were not available to Jimmy, so he decided to take guerrilla measures. Locking himself in the bathroom and taking my hairbrush in hand, he used a nail clipper to sharpen the end of each thick bristle so that when I picked up the brush the next morning, still groggy from sleep, I would dig long, pink furrows into my scalp.

I remember how exhilarating it was to hold Shonna in the palm of my hand with that story, also the care I took to fashion the anecdote when, around the ballpark that day or in the hallway during the following days at school, she asked me to repeat it. The thrill was tempered by guilt pangs: I hoped Shonna would not tell my sister how I had portrayed the family. Nevertheless, I was hooked. It was a funny story, which I sensed even as I brushed through my hair that first time, as surely as I felt the pain in my scalp.

I was certainly not the only member of my family fond of telling Jimmy stories, perhaps because Jimmy was such a reliable source of the raw material of story—conflict, humor, simple audacity. There was an edge to Jim, what I have written about elsewhere as a preternatural coolness, an instinct about what would turn a room on its collective ear. And he had the crucial courage to move on that instinct, to close the deal. While my friends and I wasted our high school nights with benign insurrection films like *Ferris Bueller's Day Off* and *Fast Times at Ridgemont High,* Jimmy, still in junior high, was memorizing long passages from the hard stuff, *Cool Hand Luke* and *Hud,* right down to the Newman smirk.

During her freshman year at Boston College, my older sister, Mary, turned a composition assignment about an interesting member of her family into a delightful essay about my brother's characteristic contrariety—how, during the year we lived in Connecticut when he was four, he insisted on wearing sweatshirts and corduroys in July and short-sleeved T-shirts in January, how he locked himself in an upstairs bathroom the night before photo day at his kindergarten and cut his own hair with dull childrens' scissors. She had her roommates call our house from Boston just so the New England girls could hear my Tennessee brother talk.

That was the lighter side of things. In fact, my brother's audacity and contrariety often bewildered my parents, who took Jimmy to several specialists to see what they could see. The doctors suggested all sorts of remedies—"time-outs," reward systems for good behavior, art lessons. One psychologist asked my mother to write a narrative of Jim's life, hoping, I guess, that the exercise would throw up on the shore some indication of the origin of the four-year-old's unruliness. What she wrote was the story of all our lives, of her marriage. Years later, I found the narrative in her stocking drawer, drafted on ruled pages in her distinctive hand. She'd clipped it to a typed copy of the essay Mary had written at BC and a photocopy of the Donald Hall poem "My Son, My Executioner." The story she wrote was full of the love I always sensed Mom felt for us, but I also heard confusion and sadness in her voice. Where had she gone wrong? Removed as I thought I was from the old trouble, it still unnerved me.

I can only guess that Ruth, my younger sister, was thinking of all of that sadness, remembering it, when she was applying for admission to graduate programs in counseling psychology. I found her letter of intent on a recent visit to my parents' house, in a drawer in her bedroom, where I happened to be sleeping. She wrote that she wanted to pursue graduate study in psychology and eventually work as a school counselor because my brother's trouble in school had so disrupted her childhood and home life. She argues that my brother had, with his outrageous behavior, made himself the center of the family, the central figure of the stories each of us told about ourselves. And we had allowed it. Ruth wanted to work with parents and children to prevent it from happening again in another family.

Since my brother was diagnosed with manic depressive illness in his mid twenties, my childhood nightmares have come back. At first the diagnosis offered the kind of relief labels always provide. We'd all been gravely worried about Jimmy—his choices became increasingly desperate and destructive as he got older. We had been given to thinking Jimmy simply had ridiculously bad judgment. Now, perhaps it was illness. A bona fide disease might also mean treatment, even a cure, and an end to our worry.

But the diagnosis worried me too. I had always mistrusted what I considered psychology's reductive, clinical coldness. It couldn't approach the enormity of a personality like my brother's, I thought. Most importantly, I was afraid I would have to reconsider my ideas about Jimmy's courage and genius. I certainly did not want Jimmy to change, invested as I was in my ideas of him.

All my siblings and I were able to get together at my parents' house in Tennessee for the better part of Christmas week a few years back, a rare treat. Even sweeter, the two new grandchildren, my parents' first, came to spend their first holiday in Martin. We were all excited to return to Christmases with small children. Jimmy was the last to arrive, as always, though he has by far the shortest commute (from Louisville, five hours by car).

One can never guess what will hold Jimmy up between his home and my parents' place—an unplanned stop at the mall in Paducah to see an old friend, a household chore that wouldn't wait. I'm not sure if he does it to just to keep us waiting (the old contrariety again, the feeling he often talked about as a little boy that he wasn't a part of the family and didn't want to be) or because something legitimately keeps him away.

Meanwhile, we waited for him, in spite of ourselves. We pretended to keep busy, or to relax, washing dinner dishes or watching television. We didn't speak of his tardiness and shushed my mother when she did. But we were waiting.

He was three and then four hours late without a call. The night turned dark and cold, and Jimmy was still out in it. I sat on a chair in the den by the back door, my anxiety having become the most petty kind of anger. I am not a man given to prayer, or I might have been praying while I sat in that chair. Instead I worry, and worried that day. I know worry is a large, elemental part of what binds me so closely to my brother Jimmy, worry that will never leave me. Brother is not an easy office to hold, which I guess I learned indirectly from my father. If my worry is a kind of hopeless praying, a futile praying without faith, then maybe my storytelling is a slightly more hopeful enterprise, a way of bearing witness, of conjuring imperiled loved ones (a loved one, in Jimmy's case, imperiled by his very nature). So I tell my brother's story, write it down.

I have never asked my brother if he minds. I know how much Jimmy admires the account he shared with me of my uncle's death—my father leaving R. L.'s hospital room that last day without a word. Jimmy loves the silence and muted emotion. Maybe my brother would like to say to me, "I wish you wouldn't tell my stories." Maybe. And maybe I'd like to ask him to lay low for a few years, take fewer chances. Come home on time.

Then the door opened, and it was Jim. Seeing my face, my worry and relief, he announced he'd have to run into the bathroom before he greeted anyone—he'd been on the road a long time. He ducked into the half-bath off the kitchen, leaving the back door wide open. I felt enveloped by the perfect egg yolk feeling again, its wholeness, and yet I thought also of the Baldwin story "Sonny's Blues": this is only a moment, and the world waits outside that back door hungry as a tiger.

By the time Jimmy emerged from the bathroom, his new wife had followed him in from the car and stood in the doorway, and my sisters and mother and the brothers-in-law and the grandchildren had come down to the back door to greet the new arrivals. We were all assembled save my father, who perhaps hadn't heard the car pull up or heard the back door open, who was perhaps somewhere else in that big house waiting for his brother to come in from a deeper cold.

# Epilogue

## *By a Song*

*Memory, like the organ, is an instrument capable of infusing the most secular music with spiritual sounds.*

James McConkey

**W**hen I was six or seven, my favorite song was John Denver's "Rocky Mountain High." I was a little confused when I heard it—figurative language still eluded me. How could a boy be born in his twenty-seven year? How could he be hanging by a song? But I didn't like the song any less for not knowing. I scratched the LP playing that same cut over and over. I tried to memorize the words, and at bedtime I sang into my pillow as much as I could remember.

I know it isn't cool to like John Denver anymore, and perhaps never was, but in the way that every younger child is hostage to the musical taste of the older sibling in the house, I was hostage to my sister Mary's record collection. My two sisters and I used to crowd around the record player when we were kids and sing along to the LPs in Mary's wire record rack: Neil Sedaka and Glen Campbell, Barry Manilow and John Denver, things Mary heard the older sisters of her school friends

The author's mother, Mary Ellen Cowser, with her children (counterclockwise from left): Bobby (age 4), Ruthie (2), Mary (6), and Jimmy (babe in arms). Taken in front of the flower bed in the side yard at 120 Virginia Street, Martin, Tenn., on the occasion of Jimmy's christening, spring 1974. From the author's family collection play at sleepovers. Mary was the only child responsible enough to collect records, the only one with any real knowledge of the world beyond our house and yard, so her music became ours, for better or worse.

After our nightly baths, Mary, Ruth, and I would slip our wet heads through the collars of our nightclothes and kneel in front of my mother's rocking chair. Mom would part my hair with a comb then pull a brush through my sisters' tangled manes. The girls teetered a bit under her gentle tugs, shifting from knee to knee as my mother brushed. Then the three of us made our way to the living room and placed ourselves on the floor in front of an old sea chest, on top of which my parents had placed the turntable. My sisters sat cross-legged in matching polyester nightgowns, threadbare at the knees. I remember the bottoms of our feet were still pink from the warm bathwater.

Of all that we listened to, I liked the folky Denver best. Hearing "Rocky Mountain High" and songs like it made me feel warm. This was what I called love when I was a boy, this warm feeling, and while the song was playing I felt it for my sisters there assembled, for my mother in the next room in front of the TV, for my father and Jimmy, just a baby then, already in bed. I felt it for the pretty ladies I knew, like my teacher Miss Webb, Mrs. Fannen from our church, Olivia Newton-John.

We speak of our waking dreams in terms of what is to come, the future, but surely we can dream about the past too. I suspect that's all memory is, a dream we dream about the way things were, no more true and no less fantastical than other kinds of dreams. True or not, it can be a kind of salvation.

The night John Denver crashed his glider Icharus-like into the Pacific, I was driving from my home in Nebraska to where my younger sister, Ruth, lives in Missouri. My wife had filed for divorce only the month before, and I was seeking the solace of family. It was 1997, my own twenty-seventh year.

I heard the news of Denver's death on a Kansas City radio station. I pulled off the interstate to find a record store and bought a John Denver cassette, the same album my sister had owned. His greatest hits. On the cover, Denver sits amid tall mountain grass, wearing a blue down vest and grinning broadly.

I had not heard "Rocky Mountain High" in a long time. I played it on the tape deck as soon as my little black car was back on the highway. There in the car, I felt the warm feeling again, simple as ever, though by that time I understood how a boy might be born again at such an age, and hoped it would happen to me. And I knew how a song could tether you to the things you love in this world: the gentle strokes of a hairbrush, warm bathwater, your little sister just a few miles farther down the road.